ETSY

MARKETING

Selling on Etsy with SEO, Facebook, Pinterest, Instagram, and Other Social Medias

By Christopher Kent

Table of Contents

INTRODUCTION

Due to the ease and convenience of online shopping, a lot of businesses are rapidly revamping themselves and trying to have an online presence. Similarly, a lot of individuals are entering into the world of buying and selling online. There are many websites and web services that allow sellers to sell their merchandise, but Etsy stands out as a unique and 'different' platform among all these services.

If you are not familiar with Etsy and how it works, this book will help you become an excellent Etsy seller and show you different methods that you can use to make your business successful. It contains many tips and tricks that are quite easy to follow, which will help you establish a stronghold as an Etsy seller.

Remember, launching your product on Etsy can be easy, but becoming popular as a seller will take a lot of effort and dedication. You need to be patient and work hard if you want to become successful.

If you are willing to learn more before you venture as a seller on Etsy, let us get started.

CHAPTER ONE

HOW TO MAKE AN ETSY BUSINESS PROFITABLE

Here are a few things you need to keep in mind when you become successful as an Etsy seller.

Finding the Right Product

Finding the right product to sell on Etsy can be as challenging as selling and marketing it. It does not matter what the nature of your business is. It can be a new store where you plan to sell your craft items, or it can be an old store where you are trying to add new items to the collection, you still need to think carefully and critically before making any solid decisions.

If you have a product in your mind and are confused about it, then these questions below can help you make a decision quickly.

Can you make it?

This is a straightforward question that rarely gets a straightforward answer. Many people tend to start a craft and homemade product business without even making the product. While dreaming is a great way to make new plans, mere dreaming will not help you fulfill them. So if you have never melted wax in your life, it is probably not the best idea to start a store specializing in candles right now.

If you do plan to make the items that you want to sell, it is highly recommended to make samples of the product before listing them on Etsy. It will help in many ways. For instance, it will allow you to solve all the problems and errors present in the product. It will also help you streamline and master the procedure so that you will make perfect products every time. If you do not follow these instructions, you will end up fixing your products right on the verge of delivery. The other advantage is that this will give you an idea of the approximate time that it takes to create a product.

Do you enjoy making it?

This is another fairly obvious question. You cannot run a business dealing with handmade products if you do not like making the products. Many people decide to sell an item because the profit margin is great and not because they enjoy making it. But if you hate making something, you will find the whole process excessively cumbersome and egregious once the orders start to roll in. This may affect the quality of the product and, ultimately, your attitude toward your business as well.

Can you find an affordable supplier for the raw materials?

A business can't work on a one-time investment. If you need to make products frequently, you need an affordable and sustainable source of raw materials. You want low prices and great products. To achieve this, it is necessary to find a good and reliable supplier so that you can make and sell your products with ease.

Instead of buying your supplies from regular stores, check the wholesale market. You can also import products from other nations in bulk.

Can you expand?

A business that deals with handmade products of one type can become quite boring after a while. But you can keep things exciting by keeping your products fresh. If your product can incorporate design variations and different materials, it will make things more exciting for both the customers and you. Variations can be of many types, including shape, size, colors, use, etc.

Do not add a lot of variety in the initial stages of the business, as this may confuse you and your customers.

Add them slowly once you get comfortable with your business.

Does it serve a purpose?

A customer will not purchase something if the product does not fulfill some need or serve a purpose. If the purpose is specific, then a lot of customers will buy it. But this does not mean that people won't buy art products. Art products, too, serve a purpose, the purpose of making the world more beautiful. But, people would rather buy something that serves a more concrete purpose. In the initial stages of your business, it is recommended to go for more practical products.

If you cannot think of any reason why a customer would want to buy your product, try to think of your target audience. For instance, if you are trying to sell book cozies, your targeted customer base will include readers of all ages who like to protect their books. By using this method, you will be able to find a purpose for your product. If the purpose doesn't seem too prominent, change the product.

Are the market conditions favorable?

Do not start a business without performing ample market research if you decide a product, conduct market research to check whether people are looking for this product or not. You can use various means for this, including the Etsy search bar, EtsyRank, the Keywords

Everywhere Chrome extension, and Google Keyword Planner. It will help you form a rough idea of how many people are looking for your item. It will also help to gauge your competition.

You should always select a product that is popular, but not too popular. This means that it should be popular, but not a lot of other sellers should already be selling it. If you still choose a saturated product, try to make your marketing and product as different as possible.

Can you legally sell it?

The legality of the product that you are trying to sell is important. You cannot sell products related to other products or licensed items, characters, logos of brands, teams, etc.

Similarly, certain products need special attention; for instance, products made for children or cosmetics. If you plan to sell these, check the rules first as safety matters.

How will you ship it?

You need to ship your products while selling on Etsy. Weigh your products immediately. You should have an idea of the cost of shipping the product.

Along with the weight of the product, you also need to check out the packing supplies that you will need. You need boxes, tapes, paper, bubble wrap, etc. Check whether your customers will be willing to pay for shipping.

If your product is too large or too heavy, your customers may or may not be willing to pay for shipping.

If you also plan to sell your products at a craft show, you need to consider how to carry them to the show. If your products can fit into bags that you can carry with you with ease, then it's great, or else you may have to use a rented vehicle.

What is your price point?

Once you have decided on the product, you need to decide the price of the product. To do this, you need to do certain calculations. For instance, you need to check how much a product costs, how much time it requires to make it, how much energy did you put into it, etc. These questions will help you decide the retail price of the product. Once you decide on a price, move on to the next step.

Do some market research. You do not want to try to undercut other sellers, as it will prove to be fatal in the long term. Your price range needs to fit within the current price range, or else potential customers will not flock to your stores fearing that your products are inferior.

If your items cost $30 to make, but almost everyone is selling the same product for $10, then you need to sit down and think. Either you will have to find a way to justify the price to the customers, or you will have to find more cost-effective ingredients.

How will you market it?

Once you have decided on the product and the retail price of the product, you need to come up with a marketing strategy. Generally, people tend to use email lists on Etsy. Others also use social media to popularize their products.

Whichever method you choose, you also need to put some time toward the designing aspect of the listing. You need to check how you plan to photograph your products etc. Making your product look attractive is important.

You will find more about marketing in the later chapters.

It is true that deciding what to sell on Etsy can be quite confusing, but if you think and plan everything properly, you will be able to come up with a profitable and sustainable business in no time.

Branding

An Etsy shop needs to look chic and noticeable so that it can attract return customers all the time. This is where branding comes into play.

Once upon a time, branding meant burning a sign into the buttocks of bulls. This was done so that people would know whose animal it was. The concept remains the same now, except it is not as violent anymore. Branding is now seen in almost every field. It can be applied to everything and everyone.

Gone are the days when brands and branding were only related to PR people and corporate offices. Now everyone has a brand, and if you understand how to use it and promote it, you will be able to run a successful business in no time.

What Is a Brand?

The brand is much more than a logo or a tagline. A brand is a perception and an expectation. Branding deals with the communication and crafting of that perception. All the things associated with brandings such as logos, jingles, ads, taglines, mascots, etc. are all just means of making the perception perceivable.

A lot of celebrities have become brands. For instance, the names of Ariana Grande, Lady Gaga, Kim Kardashian, Martha Stewart, etc. all bring specific perspectives about the individuals to your mind, respectively. This is because they own a brand of their own, or better yet, they have become a brand themselves.

Similarly, many companies such as Apple, Google, Facebook, etc. have become brands. This means that people know what to expect from these companies and where they stand on certain issues.

If you want to succeed, you need to develop a brand. This way, you can let people know things about you, such as what you care about, what you like, what you dislike, and ultimately why people should care about your products. The stronger the brand, the better the response of the customers will be. A strong brand will not only help you keep your old customers, but it will also help you invite new ones.

Defining Your Brand

Defining a brand is much more than just choosing a logo, tagline, or name for your shop. Similarly, it is more than choosing your avatar, the fonts, or the colors of your page. Everything that you decide needs to 'go' with your essence. Your every choice should represent your brand's essence.

To check the essence of the 'vibe' of your brand, use these four questions.

1. Why do you make your items?

Your story of making the products should fit in well with the image of your brand. Your authenticity and your personal touch matter a lot in businesses such as Etsy. If you have an interesting story behind the conception of your products, it will attract a lot of customers because they will understand that what they are buying is special and unique.

2. How is your product different?

You need to understand the USP or the Unique Selling Point (Proposition) of your product. Your USP allows you to tell people everything about your product in a line or two. They will know what to expect from you or your product. For instance, if you make hats, think what makes your hats different than everyone else's hats. Don't think from a seller's point of view, think from the customer's viewpoint. Customers love unique things.

3. Which words do you use to describe your items?

You need to check what kind of words you will use to describe your product or service. For instance, if you sell hats, you need to come up with adjectives that define your product and make them seem unique. You can use the 20-10-4 method to come up with these words. Think of 20 words that describe your brand or product. Then sort them down to 10. And finally, reduce them to 4. This way, you will come up with unique and excellent words. Remember "spiritual, soulful, accessible, and playful" sound and appeal people differently as compared to "sophisticated, elegant, experienced, and chic."

4. Who are your customers?

Not everyone is going to like your product, and you should not try to cater to everyone either. This is a trap that will lead to unfortunate consequences. Think about your customer base, i.e., the people who are most likely to buy your products. Think about their age, the demographics, the kind of content they like, their financial condition, their residence, etc. For instance, if your products target college students, you cannot sell them for too steep a price. Always keep your prospective customers in mind whenever you make a decision.

If you make Goth jewelry and brand it with bold pastels and an overall cheerful aura, no one will buy your products.

Building Your Brand

Once you define the attributes, the values, and the essence of your brand, you can move on to the next step. You need to build a brand message, i.e., what it stands for. To do this, here is a seven-step formula.

Clarity

You need to deliver your message in a bold and clear way. It will help you stand out, and people will remember you. Do not try to do a lot of things for a lot of people; keep it simple and elegant.

Consistency and Cohesiveness

Your brand needs to be consistent and cohesive across all the platforms that you are planning to market your product. So, for instance, if your Etsy store is Goth-like and dark, your emails, business cards, and flyers cannot be elegant and chic.

Communication

You need to communicate your brand through all the things associated with the product. For instance, your shipping and packaging material should bring out your brand. Your fonts, logo, name, and colors should align with your brand and its 'vibe.'

Competition

If you want your brand to succeed, you need to pay close attention to your competition. You need to put your brand in a competitive atmosphere if you want it to become iconic. Positioning your brand means shaping its image in the minds of your potential customer base.

First, understand what things come to the minds of customers when they think about the category of the product that you want to sell. Do they already own it? Are there any problems associated with the product that you can solve? Can you make their lives easier? Is there some sort of gap that you can fill? Can your product meet the needs that are not being met by other brands and their products?

Customers

You need to build relationships with your customers if you want your business to be sustainable. Building relationships with your customers will help you build your business as well. Know your customers - what they like or do not like, what they need, what they want, etc. Let them know that you can deliver whatever they want.

It is necessary to encourage feedback through your Etsy shop and your social media accounts. Kindness will always bring new and honest customers.

Capture Attention

Being direct, bold, helpful, and authentic can help you capture the attention of your potential customer base. Similarly, being shocking, exciting, surprising, and funny can help you too. Be whatever you can be, but remember to be memorable at all times!

SEO Optimization

Etsy-SEO

SEO or search engine optimization is essential if you want to run a successful online business. Opening an Etsy store does not take a lot of time; in fact, you can create it within a few clicks. But just opening a store does not mean that you will start reaping in cash in a day or two.

Your sale depends on whether your targeted customer base can find your products or not. This is why Etsy SEO is so important. Focusing on the optimization of your Etsy listing is essential, as it will help you make your product become more visible. A lot of views and visitors mean a lot of sales.

Optimizing products on Etsy is not a difficult task. In this section, let us have a brief look at how to optimize your products. It will help your products reach their target customers.

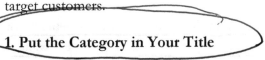

1. Put the Category in Your Title

It is necessary to include your category in the title. Customers are more likely to search the categories while looking for a particular product. For instance, if the customer is trying to buy herbal soaps, you need to put your products in the category of soaps. Do not call your product something random such as 'Herbs Wash' etc. It won't come up if customers search for herbal soaps. Instead, call it 'Herbal Wash Herbal Soap,' this way, it will show up when the customers search for it.

2. Use Long-Tail Keywords in Titles

It is true that a shorter keyword can bring in a lot of traffic, but it is not a good thing all the time. It may bring more visitors, but it may or may not bring more buyers. To attract more buyers, you need to use longtail keywords that are more specific.

Short keywords generally bring in people who are just browsing or 'window shopping.' They do not know what to buy, and most of them are just trying to pass their time. Along with this, a lot of sellers use short keywords, which means that your potential customers will get bombarded with products, and they will have to sift and sort through a lot of products to get to yours. Meanwhile, they may find another product they like, therefore increasing your sales.

People who search for longtail keywords are generally on a lookout for specific products and genuinely want to buy them. Longtail keywords reduce competition for you.

To continue with the previous example, let's say the 'customer' searches for 'soap.' He or she will be bombarded with a lot of items that he or she will have to comb through. He or she may or may not buy your product. But if you use a longtail keyword such as 'marjoram herbal soap,' it will bring fewer results. This means that the potential customer will check out your product and may even buy it. Ultimately, it all boils down to understanding and using your niche.

3. Put the Primary Keyword in the Title First

According to research, approximately the first 30 characters of your product title are the most crucial as far as SEO is concerned. This means that the first word of your title needs to be your keyword. Do not put anything random such as color, size, shape, etc. in this prime spot.

4. Include Synonyms

Many times people use different words to look for a product. To avoid losing these potential customers, you need to use some synonyms for your products as well. Put your primary keywords in the title first, but do not forget to add synonyms for the product. For instance, if you are trying to sell soaps, do add words such as 'body washes,' 'scrub,' etc. in the name. You can also include these words in the tags or product descriptions.

5. Vary Keywords for Similar Products

Etsy generally does 'declumping' to give everyone a fair chance. This means that if you sell more than one kind of soap and a customer searches for soaps, he or she will only see one (or two) items by you in the results.

This is why you should not use the same primary keyword for all your products. If you do, you will start to compete with yourself. All your products should show up in the results. To do this, try to use different variations of the keywords for similar products.

6. Don't Be Too Creative with Titles

If you are on Etsy, you are creative and unique. Many sellers try to extend their creativity to their product names as well. While it is a great way to show your uniqueness and creativity, it may have a negative effect on your sales. A creative and unique name is interesting, but it is ineffective from the point of view of the sale. People who are trying to look for products will not use unique keywords to search for them. If you plan to sell your artwork on Etsy, do not use the 'title' of the artwork as the 'title' of your listing. Instead, use the medium of the painting, such as 'acrylic on canvas,' 'oil on canvas,' etc. You can put the 'title' of the artwork in the description of the listing.

7. Use Keywords in Tags

You can use 13 tags to tag your items. This is a great opportunity for you to attract customers. Each tag has a limit of 20 characters. Think as many search terms as you can to make your endeavor profitable. If you plan to sell watches, use keywords such as timepieces, wristwatch, men's watch, antique watch, metal watch, 1925 silver watch, engraved watch, gift watch, etc.

Etsy does not allow you to repeat attributes and categories because they are already used in the search results, so keep your tags as specific as possible.

Using Social Media

Social media promotions can be confusing if you are a beginner. This section will help you decide which social media to focus on to make your shop pop.

Marketing Social Media

Social media is a great and cost-effective tool for promotions, especially for small business owners. With the help of social media marketing, a seller can not only connect with his or her customers, but he or she can also build brand awareness and can meet new potential customers as well.

All forms of social media channels come with their pros and cons. This is why you need to change your promotion style according to the channel. Before you begin a social media promotion campaign, you need to check what kind of strategies work on the platform that you plan to use.

Here is a small list of things that you should keep in mind.

Facebook

- **Pros**

It is great for video content, especially the "Live" feature. It can also be used for customer service, photo collections, FB messaging, direct contact with customers, connecting with people, sharing product listings, and reaching out to a variety of audiences.

- **Cons**

Not great for reaching out to teens and other young demographics.

Instagram

- **Pros**

Instagram is great for cross-promotion, visually bold appeal, finding and attracting influences, behind-the-scene action, giveaways, IG Stories, reaching young demographics, etc.

- **Cons**

Instagram is not the best platform for overtly promotional content.

Pinterest

- **Pros**

Pinterest is home to on-trend products, trend lovers, inspirational boards, creative thinking, visual thinkers, etc.

- **Cons**

Pinterest can be too time-consuming.

If you are a newbie to the world of social media, it is recommended to promote your shop through only one channel in the beginning. It will keep you from being overwhelmed. You can begin with a channel that suits your current needs and the one that you can handle with ease. If you are a social media nut, you can begin your promotions through all the channels all at once. Use the power of social media to its full extent to reap the benefits fully.

Facebook for Connecting with Customers

One of the best sites to connect with your potential buyers who are already familiar with your products and brands is Facebook. There are many different tools available on Facebook that can help you promote your brand. For instance, the "Live" option can help you connect with your customers directly. It can also help let them know what new developments are going on with your shop.

Facebook can also be used to share information about new products and give customers sneak peeks of your new products. You can use Facebook to gain feedback from your customers. It can be used to show your customers some behind-the-scenes action.

If you are new to the world of Facebook promotions, do not dive indirectly and stay in your comfort zone. Promote your content to the people who know you, such as friends and family. This way, you will get instant feedback, and you can change things if they do not make sense.

Pinterest for the Curator

If you love creating mood boards and like to horde images, Pinterest can be a boon for you.

All other social media platforms are more focused on the present (and perhaps the past), but Pinterest is focused on future events. Business owners who are trend-forward can use Pinterest to register their inspirations and ideas. They can also learn a lot of new color schemes and trends.

Instagram for the Visual Storyteller

If you are high on visuals, Instagram can be the best deal for you. Instagram can be the best tool for you if you are social and like images. Instagram is not only very visual, but it is also quite interactive. You can share a lot of images such as your behind-the-scenes process, the personal ideas of your brand, etc.

You can also display pictures of your works in progress, or they give sneak peeks of your products. Along with this, you can share tours of your studio on the Stories feature. You can also use creative hashtags to connect with targeted buyers.

If you are still confused about social media, fret not. Just try out a few services until you make a decision. You will find out more about social media marketing and specific social platforms in the next chapters.

CHAPTER TWO

DRIVING TRAFFIC WITH SEO

Tag and Title

Using tags and titles on Etsy is a great (and free) way to attract more shop traffic towards your shop and increase your sales as well. Using strong tags and titles will help your products to get noticed by not only the Etsy search but other search engine giants as well. The title is crucial because it sends your first impression to the customer. Tags are important because they help your product reach a large audience.

Titles and tags often require a lot of trial and error, and they are quite confusing as well. This chapter will help you avoid these basic mistakes and improve your Etsy sales in no time. Here are some tips to get you started.

Forget Being Grammatically Correct

If you love being grammatically correct all the time, you will have let go of this habit (at least in the case of Etsy). All top sellers are aware that you need to put targeted keywords in the title to attract the right kinds of buyers. But putting these keywords in titles will often mean grammatically incorrect titles.

Many times Etsy sellers try to use grammatically correct sentences. They use filler words such as 'the,' 'of,' 'and,' etc. But these words take up a lot of unnecessary space out of the 140 characters that are available to users. It is necessary to use this limited set of characters as judiciously as possible. Delete any filler words and only add words that your customers may input in the search bar.

Another problem that new sellers face is naming their products in a weird manner. If you name your product line something exotic, your customers will not find them with ease. Your title should contain some targeted keywords so that your customers can find the products.

Place Your Strongest Keywords at the Front of Your Title

As said in the previous chapter, the first 30-45 characters in the title are the main characters. You need to input your most crucial keywords here. If you do not know which keywords to use here, just check the stats of your product. Use the top 3 keywords and then arrange them in front of your title.

The initial keywords in the title can also help your products turn up on search engines such as Google.

Your second most important keywords should follow your most important keywords.

Use All 140 Characters of Your Title

Do not skimp words; use all 140 characters available for your title. As said above, the first 30-45 characters need to be your most popular keyword. You can use the final characters for the longtail keywords.

Longtail keywords, as the name suggests, are long, and generally contain specific words in relation to your product. The specificity of these keywords allows customers to find your products with ease.

To choose longtail keywords, check out your stats. Here you will get some ideas about your potential customers' searches. Adjust these words into the second part of the title. It is also recommended to use the other longtail keywords in tags.

If you are listing a new product and have no longtail keywords to look for, check your competitor's profile. Search for a product similar to your product on Etsy. Check the first three listings and use the keywords used by these listings. These can be used in your tags as well.

Match Etsy Tags with Targeted Keywords

Visit your stats for every product on Etsy individually and check the keywords that are used generally by people. This can be done for all kinds of listings that are at least in the system for a month. Add the keywords that are high-volume to your tags and get rid of all the tags that do not bring any results or inquiries.

If a longtail keyword is too long, you can divide it into two tags as well. It will have the same impact.

Use Different Keywords

If there is more than one item that falls under the same category or that are similar, do not use the same titles for them. Yes, it may seem easy to just copy your titles, but this will lead to problematic sales. Etsy curates and manages searches differently. This means that if you have multiple products with similar titles, only a couple of them will show up in the search results. If you want all your products to show up in search results, you need to use similar but different tags. Diversifying your keywords is the best way to get new customers and attract buyers. This way, you can display your products to a lot of potential customers.

This does not mean that you should change your titles and tags all the time. You can use different longtail keywords. It will help you come up with new and great keywords.

Revise Your Listing

After every two months, it is recommended to revise your listings. You should revise the tags and the title to attract new customers.

Check the stats of your product on Etsy and check the keywords. You may surprisingly find new keywords that people have been using to search for your product.

Check the stats of any low performing listing every couple of weeks and freshen it up from time to time. If a listing is performing particularly badly, revise the longtail keywords and place the high-volume keywords in the front of the title.

Keywords Research

People prefer to use Etsy over other online retail stores because they know that they will find something special on it. By typing just a few words into the search bar, the users can find anything they want. Etsy search is designed in such a way that it can help all kinds of shoppers to find whatever they are looking for.

The Essentials

The keywords that the seller uses in titles, tags, attributes, and categories all work simultaneously to help the customer find the products. Whenever the user searches something, and it matches the keywords used by a particular seller, the products have the possibility of showing up in the search results.

Etsy search collects all the listings that contain the keywords that the customer puts in the search bar. Then these listings are ranked according to the keywords and relevancy. This means if the seller uses a strong keyword in his or her product listing, the listing will have more chances to show up in the search results. Let us have a look at some common tips that can help your products to show up in search results effectively.

Categories

Categories are quite similar to tags, and in categories, you can add a variety of options that are relevant to your requirements. Adding specific categories can enhance search engine results. Whenever you add sub-categories in your listings, the items automatically get segregated in all the categories that you have added in a nested form.

As categories are like tags, you should not repeat the date used in tags. Keep your attributes, categories, and tags all different. This way you can make your product really popular.

Attributes

Attributes, as the name suggests, are extra details that you can add to your listings. This can be done once you choose a category. Attributes can really help your products pop and standout between hundreds of search results in the same category. Attributes include paint, size, shape, and many others.

It should be understood that all attributes act like tags; this is why you should only use relevant options even if they do not make semantic or syntactical sense. This means that even if your product is turquoise-colored, you should still add blue to your listing. Similarly, if you put in 'nature-inspired' for your product, you should also add 'trees and plants' as attributes.

There is no necessity to add tags that are totally similar to the attributes. For instance, if you write 'blue shades' to the attributes, you do not need to add 'blue shades' as a tag once again. You can add multi-word descriptive tags, though. So you can add 'elegant fur blue shades' as a tag.

Titles

Keywords are important in the case of titles as well. These are necessary because they allow the consumer to search for your products with ease. But titles, while important, are not the most important thing for Etsy, they are just one of the many keywords that Etsy searches for.

A seller should always write a clear, short, and descriptive title for the ease of convenience of the customer. Always add your most prominent keywords to the front of the title. You are also allowed to use punctuation marks in your title to separate the phrases; it will not affect your search in a negative way.

Do remember to add the most descriptive keywords in your title. Also, remember that you are trying to sell your products to a person and not a computer and write your titles accordingly.

If the seller adds a lot of keywords to the title, it may confuse the customer, or may even put them off. But if the seller does not add enough keywords, the product may not turn up in the search. This is why the seller needs to seek the middle ground and come up with a title that not only contains all the keywords but is comprehensible as well.

Tags

A seller can add 13 phrases to his or her listing to describe the product. Each tag that the seller adds to the listing makes his or her product more attractive and search worthy. The seller should spread out his or her tags as much as possible. Let us have a look at some dos and don'ts of tagging:

Tagging Do's

1. Use all the tags available as each tag is, in a way, an opportunity for you to sell the product.

2. Use multi-worded tags. You can add tags that are 20 characters long. You can use multiple phrases in tags. For instance, if you add a 'custom wallet' as one tag, you will be able to save the space of another one.

3. Check your Shop Stats. Check out the tags that are not receiving enough traffic. Change them around.

4. Use synonyms. If you sell bed covers, you need to tag your product with bedsheets and bed covers both. This way, a customer will be able to look for your product by using synonyms as well. Etsy can take into account the 'jewelry' and 'jewelry' confusion, but it won't consider all the synonyms on its own.

5. Understand and use regional phrases. If you plan to sell flip-flops throughout the world, it is necessary to add all the regional varieties to the tags. You need to add 'thongs,' 'thongs sandals,' 'slippers,' 'floaters,' etc. to the listing.

6. Use longtail keywords. Instead of using simple and especially generic keywords for your products, use less popular phrases that describe your product to T. Target, the shopper who knows what they are looking for.

Tagging Don'ts

1. A seller can use 13 tags in a listing. All these tags should always be unique. Do not use repeated tags. Make them unique. For instance, if you add 'leopard print' as a tag, do not add tags such as 'leopard art' 'leopard skin art.' Diversify your tags as much as possible.

2. Never repeat attributes and categories. The attributes and categories both function like tags. Do not add the phrases that you have used in categories as tags again.

3. Do not use misspellings. Many times sellers try to add misspellings to their tags because they are worried about misspellings from the customers' side. This is a valid concern, but Etsy takes into account all the common misspellings. It will direct customers to your listing even if you make a minor typographical error.

4. Do not add tags in different languages. The tags and titles should both be in the language that you used to set up your shop. Etsy translates the tags and titles on its own. Or you can translate the listings on your own if you desire to do so.

5. Do not worry about adding plurals to the listings. Etsy only looks at the root words while searching for listings. This means that even if you add 'diamonds' or 'diaries' to your tags, Etsy will still direct customers looking for 'diamond' and 'diary' to your listing.

How to Think about Tags

As said previously, it is crucial to use all the 13 tags and make them unique. To make your tags unique, you need to think about what makes your products unique as well. It will allow you to think about what shoppers think about your products. As the character limit of the tags is just 20 characters, you will have to be as creative as possible. If you try to use a keyword phrase that is longer than 20 characters, it is recommended to divide them into more than one keyword. Breaking the phrase into multiple tags will not affect your listing negatively. But do not divide the phrases into single-word keywords, as they will take up unnecessary space.

Descriptive tags that are accurate and clear will help you describe your products thoroughly. But there are various other kinds of tags that you can use.

Descriptive

The categories added to the listings need to describe what the product is. There should also be some tags that should describe your product in your own words. Just remember that it is better to use multi-word phrases instead of using individual words.

Examples: vintage cat brooch, reusable envelope dots, polka ceramic cup, set of eight coasters

Materials and Techniques

The seller knows his or her product better than anyone else. Try to add highlights that make your product unique. For instance, if you sell customized items, it is crucial to add phrases that will convey this message to your potential customers. Try to be as specific as possible.

Examples: Customized wallet, engraved keychain, reclaimed wooden frame, custom handkerchiefs

Who it's for-

Make your content unique and customized. Your potential customer should be able to check your product and know for whom it is made. Think of your potential customer in such a way that he or she is trying to gift your product to someone else.

Examples: Gifts for girlfriends, gifts for weddings, gifts new moms, professor gift

Shopping Occasions

An excellent seller always puts himself or herself in the shoes of the customer. He or she understands the various occasions when people tend to buy things. For instance, imagine that you are hosting a party. What kind of things will you search on Etsy to make your party memorable? Describe your things using these keywords.

A quick reminder: Occasion attributes need to incorporate descriptions that are relevant to the occasion. This does not mean that you cannot add tags to products that are not strictly meant for these occasions but can be used thanks to their relevancy. For instance, while stockings are strictly not made for Christmas, they can be used for the holiday. To make them more relevant, you can add the word Christmas in front of stockings so that the customers will be able to find the products with ease.

Solution-Oriented

You can also make your product's solution-oriented and tag them similarly. For instance, if your products can help people in one way or another, it can be a great gift to the person. Certain solution-oriented products include headbands, indoor pots, lunch boxes, etc.

Examples: closet organization, lunch box decal, workout headbands, and indoor garden

Style

People tend to have a personal aesthetic or style that helps them make proper decisions regarding their clothes because people like to show off their style and charisma to the world. You can tap into this and can adjust your tags accordingly. You can use these tags to reflect various style choices and preferences.

For instance, you can use style palette, time period, aesthetics, etc. that match the products that you plan to sell. You can combine the name of the product with the style or time period to make a multi-phrasal tag.

Examples: Minimalist ring, art deco lamp, rustic wall decor, typographic print, etc.

Size

The size of the products can also help you decide the attributes of your keyword. For instance, you can add tags that describe the shape and size of your product.

Examples: Deep basket, small beach tote, teen pants, large silver hoops

Tools for updating your titles and tags

If you want to use the above tips in your shop, there are some methods that you can use to make rapid changes. You can either remove or add a tag from many different listings simultaneously by checking the boxes on these listings in the Shop Manager option. Just click on Editing

Option, followed by Edit tags. You can also edit your tags and titles with the help of the Quick Edit tool. You will be able to make quick updates without having to click on each listing separately.

Ranking

Etsy is a great eCommerce platform that is brilliant for sellers who plan to sell unique products. It is now considered to be the fastest-growing e-store all around the world.

If you want to become a successful seller on Etsy, you need to use the Etsy SEO service and strategies carefully. In the past, the process of optimizing Etsy listings was simple. This way, sellers could ensure the higher rankings of their listings. Sellers only had to fill some key areas in the listing forms, but now times have changed because the technology has evolved. The search algorithm for Etsy is revamped and is now controlled by AI or Artificial Intelligence. This has resulted in a smarter search engine, which is great for buyers but not so great for vendors. But this does not mean that the vendors cannot use the new search engine. You just need to update yourself and your techniques.

How Does Etsy Search Work?

Before moving on how to optimize the search engine, let us first have a look at the functioning of the Etsy search engine in brief.

1. Tag and Title

The current search option of Etsy is like Google. In Google, the title and tags of a product need to match the search query of the consumer. Similarly, the search query of an Etsy customer needs to match the seller's tags and titles as well. If the search terms do not match or not present at all, the listing will not be included in the results as well.

How to solve it?

It is true that sellers cannot control some ranking factors, but they can always conduct research and curate the product description in such a way that it will include all the tags, the title, attributes, and descriptions properly. Instead of focusing on the listing, in the beginning, you should always focus on the description of the product.

Let us have a look at some simple tips that can help you create a comprehensive and useful product description:

a. The product title needs to be search-friendly. If the product has the exact (matching) term, then the term should be given a high priority. Always check the product descriptions of similar products sold by other sellers. Try to write a product description that is similar to these descriptions.

b. Always try to incorporate relevant keywords as well as longtail query terms in your description. As said above, sellers can add 13 keywords in their tags. Use all these.

c. While you can make a 140 characters long title, the search generally shows only the first 55 characters. This means you're your keyword needs to be in the first 55 characters. This will not only help the customers to know the nature of your product, but it will also help with the integrated Google Shopping experience.

d. Tags and titles are used by Etsy search engines. These search terms are relevant intentionally as well as commercially. Use these tags as much as possible.

2. Attribute Relevance

Attributes are relevant as far as search is considered. Along with tags and titles, attributes are important as well, as buyers often tend to search for products using terms like 'Black dress shoes,' 'Small skirt,' etc.

How to solve it?

You should always choose the category of the product first and the sub-category of the product later. It will help you choose the types of attributes for your products. These attributes can include size, color, and many other things as well. It is recommended to select as many correct and relevant attributes as possible. These attributes should be related to the product that you are listing. It will help you to expose your product to a multitude of customers.

Choosing the relevant categories is important because it can help the buyers to find your products with ease. It is crucial to add specific information to your products. This way, the users will find your products with ease, and they will buy them immediately.

3. Quality of Product Listing

The more favorites, clicks, and purchases a listing receives, the more will be its chances to do well in the search option. This factor is known as the 'listing quality' of the product. But with new technology, listing quality is becoming obsolete, and Etsy has neutralized it. In new shops, it plays little to no role in search results.

How to solve this?

Etsy uses an automated option in this case. The products that get the most attention, i.e., more clicks and purchases and which have high conversion rates, are given preference over other products. Do pay attention to the uniqueness of your products. You need to work hard. The quality of your products needs to be excellent.

Tips:

- Always make sure that your buyers are getting an excellent experience.

- Ask your buyers to leave positive reviews on the product pages.

- Add the seller's policy clearly in the About Us section of your shop.

- Do not price your products too high or too low. It will lead to fewer clicks. Conduct some research to check your competitions' prices. Come up with proper prices after research.

4. Regular Updates

Etsy's search engine algorithm generally prefers the product that was updated recently. It pays ample attention to the listing or relisting dates of the products.

How to solve this?

To keep your listings fresh, update the title, details, and tags of your products frequently. It will help you keep your content up-to-date and fresh all the time.

5. Shop Location

Etsy search takes into account the shop location of the vendor to make search results more suitable for the customer. This means if the customer searches for a product in Australia, he or she will not see the store situated in the United States on the first page of the search results. The shop location needs to be proper to make the rankings perfect.

How to solve this?

The main motive behind this location business is to ensure quick delivery to shoppers. Third-party vendors have no option to deal with this, as they have no control over this phenomenon.

6. Artificial Intelligence

According to Etsy, they are trying to make their search system more intelligent now. This way, the searches will be better and more relevant. They have incorporated various factors in the search results such as preferences, time of the day, etc. This is good news for buyers because it will help them to find products with ease, but it is bad news for vendors because these provisions may lead to selling and tagging problems. This because whenever the user types in a keyword in the search option, he or she will not see the same results every time.

How to solve this?

It is true that the latest technology is making things difficult for vendors on Etsy, but there are certain tricks and tips that can help vendors to keep their business afloat and thriving. Let us have a look at these tips:

- **Etsy Rank**

This is a rank checker tool that can search Etsy for all your items and can filter personalization results as well. It is available for free. It can filter bulk reports as well.

- **Etsy Stats**

The sellers are able to use the 'Search Terms' section to check which keywords the customers are using to look for your products.

7. Listing Language

When a person signs up on Etsy, it is crucial to list products in the language of his or her shop. All the listing information for all the products needs to be in the native language of the Marketplace. So, if the Marketplace is in the French language, then do not use English Keywords, or these keywords will not be recognized by the website.

How to solve it?

The listing information that the seller puts on Etsy should always be the same as the language of the Marketplace.

8. Relevant Linking

Links are good for the search engine ranking. It is recommended to link your shop page to the policies and the products listed on the Etsy Marketplace. Your shop page should consist of the following information: Shop Name: The name of the shop.

- Shop Description: What your shop entails and what you plan to sell.

- Sales Count: How many sales you made in the past.

- Start Date: When you opened your shop.

The shop page information is available at Marketplace. This information is great because it allows you to enhance the visibility of your product and promote your shop as well. Similarly, it will also help your products to become more popular.

CHAPTER THREE

FACEBOOK MARKETING

Nowadays, people are always on a lookout for promoting their products on various sites and services. But many sellers who own a small-scale business do not want to spend a lot of money on this. Facebook, along with various other social media platforms, can help you do this, along with various other things with ease.

Facebook is now being used by many eCommerce business ventures, including Etsy shop owners throughout the world to promote their products without spending a lot of money on advertising. Anyone can use Facebook ads to grow their business if they learn how to use it. You just need to learn how to use the basics of the platform.

This chapter will serve as a guide for all the people who want to start using Facebook as a way to increase their business. Facebook, if used properly, can improve your business.

Why Use Facebook for Advertising?

There are many different options available on the market that can be used by small-scale business owners, such as Etsy shop owners to promote their products. But Facebook is perhaps the most popular one because it has these three characteristics:

1. Driving Traffic from an Active and Engaged User Base

Facebook is a social website where people tend to connect to their friends and family. A lot of people hate Facebook because it is extremely addictive. But this addictive nature of Facebook can prove to be an asset to you. According to reports, around two billion people use

Facebook actively each month. These users spend more time on Facebook as compared to any other social media site. With this, Facebook now also owns Instagram and Messenger. Both these mobile apps are extremely popular as well and are good for advertisements as well. You can divert these people towards your business page and, in the process, increase your business.

2. Targeting Customers

With the help of Facebook, you can target your customers using various parameters such as their age, gender, and various other demographics as well. This is because Facebook is designed in a manner that people tend to share their personal updates on it. These personal updates include vacation pictures, songs that they like, movies that they watch, etc. All the connections and likes that these people create on Facebook are used to generate a user profile that can be used to create targeted ads. Facebook advertisers can then create ads in such a way that their targeted demographic will want to buy these products. This way, your product will reach a lot of people and increase your sales as well.

3. Generating Brand Awareness

Nowadays, a lot of businesses have an Instagram or a Facebook business account. This way, they can connect with their customers and fans through social media.

Once you decide to use Facebook to promote your shop, you need to create a social page for your brand. This way, you can expose your brand to a lot of new people. Social media can help you reach new people and new potential customers as well.

Step 1: Setting Up Your Facebook Business Manager

While many people start using Facebook advertising in the beginning, they give up soon because they think that it involves a lot of effort. But, if done properly, Facebook advertising does not require a lot of effort. Many people get overwhelmed by Facebook's multitude of options. These options confuse many people, and they end creating strange ads.

To begin things properly, you need to set up your Business Manager account properly.

Business Manager is the special option available on Facebook that contains your business page, your ad account, and all the other tools relevant to your advertisement purposes.

To create your Business Manager account, visit business.facebook.com, and click Create Account. Here Facebook will ask for the name of your business, followed by your business page details, your email address, and your name. If you have not created a page for your business already, do it immediately.

After this, you will have to create an advertising account. You can also add an already existing account. To add an account, you need to use the Business Settings account available in the Business Manager Menu. To do this, just click on Accounts, followed by Ad Accounts. You will be presented with multiple options for adding a new or an existing account. If you are new to the world Facebook ads, just click on Create a New Ad account. Follow the steps carefully.

Once you create your Facebook business account properly, you will be presented with a screen that is known as the advertising hub. Here you can view all the different and relevant business areas on Facebook.

Step 2: Installing the Facebook Pixel

One severe problem that many new Facebook advertisers face is of 'presence' of ads. This means that there is no way to check whether your ads are working or not. You can set up advertising campaigns and can boost posts using Facebook Ads Manager, but it won't help you check the relevance of the ads. To do so, you need to install the Facebook pixel. Here you can check whether you ad really helped you get sales or not.

The Facebook pixel serves as a link between Facebook ads and your Etsy shop or your special website. It is a tracking code that you need to create in the Business Manager account. It can then be added to your website before purchasing the ads. This code will allow you to see all the visitors (and their actions) on your website through Facebook ads. The pixel will help you understand which ads brought people to your page, which ads made them buy things, and which ads did not work at all. It will allow you to make better ads that will tap into your potential customer base properly.

Step 3: Creating Facebook Audiences

It is necessary to learn how to target your core audience carefully with the help of Facebook advertising. Facebook has billions of users around the world. You need to work hard to target your customer base carefully.

You can create a target list of people in your Business Manager. You just need to access the Audience section in Business Manager. There are many different options available in this section through which you can define your customer base. All these options can be divided into two sections: Prospecting and Retargeting. Let us have a look at both of these ones by one.

Retargeting: Converting Warm Audiences

A person who visited your website or your Instagram and added something to the cart is more likely to buy something from you as compared to other people. But you need to push these people a little to encourage them to make the purchase.

Many times when you browse the website or the page of a brand, Facebook tends to show you ads related to the brand. This is known as retargeting. It is one of the best and effective features of Facebook advertisings.

It is possible to create a retargeting audience with the help of the Custom Audience feature. This feature is situated in the Audience section of the Business Manager option. Custom Audience allows you to use all the data captured with the help of Facebook pixels along with business pages.

A lot of different sources are made available to the seller when he or she decides to create a Custom Audience. The three major sources include website traffic, customer file, and engagement. Let us have a look at these three ones by one.

1. Customer file

In this source, you can upload a list of phone numbers, email addresses, and all other relevant contact information that you collect from leads or customers. Facebook will then match these parameters with its users so that you can target the audience who will be interested in your products. Using the customer file to create an audience is a great way to re-engage past customers and meet new customers as well. You can also reach the customers who have not made a purchase yet using this method.

2. Website Traffic

This source allows you to create a retargeting list that can help visitors to reach your web page. In this method, you can create lists of many different sizes. The size of these lists depends on the pages visited by your customers and the actions taken by them. Generally, these lists contain all the users who have visited your page in the past month. It also includes customers who added some products to their cart in the last week.

3. Engagement

If you have created an active Instagram or Facebook page for your business, you often get sharers, commenters, and likers. You should try to use these for your own benefit as well. To do this, just click on Select Engagement from the Custom Audience option. Here you can create a list of various types of engagement that can be retargeted. This service will help you target all the people who have ever liked or commented on your page by checking whether they will be interested in purchasing products from you, or not.

Prospecting: Finding New Customers

After the retargeting, the other crucial method of Facebook advertising is prospecting.

While retargeting allows you to contact people who know your business or have bought something from you in the past, prospecting allows you to contact new users. This way, you can find new customers and increase your sales with ease.

In terms of advertising, looking for new customers is also known as 'prospecting.' In this method, you create ads that target people who have never interacted with your business or have never bought anything from you. For medium and small-sized businesses, this includes almost billions of active users present on Facebook. It is impossible to target all these people, which is why you need to narrow the list down.

Facebook has made a couple of tools available to users to make this process simple. Let us have a look at these tools individually.

1. Lookalike Audiences

Facebook can create a list of prospective buyers for you by using the list of your past customers. This method is known as Lookalike Audiences. Facebook can use the data present in Custom Audiences to create a new audience to find a new audience that shares similarities with your old or existing customers.

It is possible to create Lookalike Audiences using a variety of options available in Custom Audiences.

2. Interests, Behaviors, and Demographics

If you do not possess a list of your past customers, you cannot create a Lookalike Audience. You can still use Facebook's behaviors, interests, and demographic data to solve this problem. You just need to use the saved audience option for this.

Let us have a look at all the above categories one by one:

- Interests include all the content and Facebook pages that users interact with. This includes music groups, book-related pages, adventure sports, etc.

- Behaviors include all the actions that users perform on Facebook. This includes getting married, moving to a new city, joining a new institute or job, etc.

- Demographics include the user's profile information, including their education, gender, etc.

You will have the option of checking many different audiences to test from. This can prove to be quite confusing, but you can narrow these options by identifying the categories for testing. To make this process simple, you can use the Audience Insights option that is available in the Business Manager section, which is available in the Plan section of the main menu. Here you can use your Facebook page and can also input the demographic information about your customer base. This tool will then show a lot of information about your potential customer base, including what pages they generally like and spend time on, what devices do they use to access Facebook, where do they live, what are their likes, etc.

This information collected by Audience Insights can then be used to find new interests and can ultimately be used to target new customers as well.

The behavior, interests, and demographics of audiences are quite extensive, and you will find thousands or even millions of users online with similar interests, so it is recommended to check the above three criteria personally. It will allow you to narrow your ads even more, and you will be able to target the audience properly.

Step 4: Creating a Facebook Campaign

The ads present on the user's feeds are generally accompanied by the word 'sponsored.' But you will be surprised to know that these ads are just the tip of the iceberg.

If you want to promote your products successfully on Facebook, you need to create an ad campaign. The ads mentioned above are just a part of these campaigns. In fact, in every single campaign, there exists a multitude of ads. Here you can choose your budget, your audience, and then your target group. You can also select which ads the users will see. As a single campaign contains many different ad sets, you can check the ads and the set of ads on different groups of people to check their effectiveness and relevance.

Choosing an Objective for Your Campaign

Before creating an ad campaign, you need to form the objective of the ad campaign.

To create an ad campaign, go to the Ad Manager tab, which is present in your Business Manager account. Here click on Create Button. Here, you will have to insert an objective for your ad campaign.

Generally, objectives for Facebook ads can be divided into three categories; these are:

- Consideration

- Awareness

- Conversion

Each category contains a list of many different options, for instance, video views, traffic, product catalog sales, etc. You need to consider the motto of your business and what you plan to achieve from your ad campaign. The answers to these questions will help you choose an excellent ad campaign manifesto. Here are some examples that will prove how different goals can affect the objective of your ad campaign.

If you plan to increase sales in your shop, you need to set your objective to Conversions.

● If you find it difficult to sell products through your shop, you should choose the Add to Cart button. Generally, this objective is more cost-effective as compared to Conversions.

● If you are not selling a product yet, but just want to create a buzz or awareness of your product, you can do so using the Brand Awareness objective. This is also a cost-effective option.

● If you are selling products but don't have enough Traffic or are finding it difficult to drive traffic towards your web page, then you can choose the Traffic objective. This will allow you to create a retargeting list.

● If you want more comments, likes, and shares on your social media posts, use the Engagement objective.

Whatever objective you choose, Facebook will always charge you according to the number of impressions or the number of people that saw and interacted with your ads. It is crucial for you to communicate your objective so that your ads will be optimized according to your ultimate goals. If you select Traffic but want to increase purchases, you may or may not get your desired results because your chosen objective does not match your goals.

Before creating ad sets, you need to name your ad campaign as well. It is not a thing that can be overlooked.

Naming your ad campaigns can help you keep things sorted. It will reduce the confusion and also help you keep your account well organized. By naming your ad campaigns properly, you can check out their objectives instantaneously. Your campaign names can also help you with your target audience at one glance.

How you choose your names depends on you. The only thing that you need to remember is to name campaigns in such a way that you will be able to navigate the campaigns with ease.

Step 5: Setting up your Ad Sets

Once you choose the objective of your ad campaign, you need to set the ad set level. Here you are presented with many different options, including:

- Which audience you plan to target

- Your budget

- Where do you want to put your ads in the network of Facebook and Facebook products?

You will have to provide various data, including the type of events and objectives. For instance, if you have chosen Conversion as the objective to gain new sales, you will have to select the conversion event that will match with your goals.

Setting Your Budget and Schedule

The next crucial set for ad sets is the budget. You need to input your budget and then choose whether the budget will be a lifetime budget or a daily budget. Choosing your budget can be quite confusing, to make the process simple, consider the following things:

- Your budget for marketing. If you cannot afford a lot or marketing, do not waste money. Find cost effective methods.

- Cost of production: If your production takes a lot of money, adjust your marketing accordingly.

- Cost of Product: If you plan to sell your product at a higher price, you will have to keep your marketing budget high as well.

- Your Objective: Generally sales-focused objective needs a lot of marketing budget as compared to awareness-focused objectives.

- Customer Acquisition Cost: You need to take into account your average customer acquisition cost. It will help you set up your budget properly.

Remember to give a fair shot to Facebook ads by allotting them a decent budget. If you really want to achieve your goals, you should take marketing seriously. Once the ads go live, you need to allow some budget and time to the 'learning phase' of Facebook. In this phase, the algorithm of Facebook checks your data and starts optimizing to achieve your objective successfully.

Audience

In the ad sets, you will have to choose and refine a retargeting or a prospecting list that you created in the Audiences section. Choosing the gender, location, ages, and languages option can help you narrow down your audience. It will also allow you to test your ad sets with different demographics.

At the bottom of the page, you will also find an option through which you can conduct detailed targeting with the help of Facebook interests, behaviors, and demographics. Here you can choose categories that can help you create a new audience that can be layered on the top of your current audience.

At the ad set level, it is also possible to target people on the basis of a Connection. This can be done by tapping into the list of people who like your business, app, page, and events. You can even entail their friends. If you have a lot of people who come under these categories, the targeting based connections can help your app significantly.

Placements

Ad sets also allow you to control and choose where you want your ad to appear. As mentioned earlier, a lot of popular apps, including Instagram, are owned by Facebook. Ad sets allow you to place your ads in these apps as well. It is solely up to you where to put the ads.

Step 6: Choosing Your Creative (Your Ad)

The last step is to create your Facebook ad in a creative way. The advertising on Facebook as a platform is quite different than other traditional forms of advertising.

When you want to create an ad on Facebook, you are presented with options to select the Instagram account or Facebook business page where you can present your ads. This is great for your brand because it can help you create awareness of your brand. Even if it is not your main provision, it can still help you create a great brand.

Retargeting with Dynamic Product Ads

The dynamic product ads are used heavily on Facebook. If you have ever checked an online store where the page retargeted you to similar products that you viewed in the past, this is a form of dynamic ad. These ads use the data presented by Facebook pixel data along with the Facebook product catalog.

Step 7: Optimizing your Facebook Campaigns

One of the first and major steps that you need to take to make a successful Facebook ad is creating the ad campaign. You also need to learn how to optimize and monitor the performance and progress of the campaign. It will help you achieve great success. It is recommended to check your Facebook ads at least once a day. If you can do it more than once a day, that's great!

It can be quite tempting in the beginning to make changes in the targets or even switch off the ads completely if you do not see purchases in a couple of days, but it does not matter. You just need to be as patient as possible.

Facebook ads need a lot of optimization time. This is important because the algorithm requires a lot of time to optimize things carefully. If you want to switch off your ad, wait for a while, and check whether it gets 1000 impressions or not. If it does not receive 1000 impressions, then you can either invest more money, or you can always shut it down. Just give it ample time.

Creating a Funnel

Remarketing and Prospecting are two important tools that can help you get a good audience, but you need to use them together to make them even better. When both these are used together, a 'funnel' is formed.

A funnel is an interesting marketing strategy that works off the premise that not a lot of people on the market are ready to buy something right at the moment. The funnel marketing strategy uses this concept to create a marketing plan that is tailored to the audience and their purchasing interests. It allows you to target your audience and become familiar with your product and your brand.

Creating a funnel on Facebook can be done with the help of a cold audience, using options such as Lookalike Audience. Or you can also use the behavior-based audience in the campaign. Then you can retarget the visitors that you receive from the last campaign to another campaign.

With time, your budget will increase, and similarly, the funnel system will become more intricate and complex. This way, you will be able to target a multitude of customers within the funnel with ease.

If any time you feel that Prospecting is not creating a lot of profit for your business, you should choose a high funnel objective, which will be less expensive. This includes traffic objective or objectives. You can create a list of prospects to retarget in another campaign.

It will lead to the formation of a funnel using your Facebook ads. This way, you will be able to target many different demographics of the audience, and your purchases will increase.

Start Using Facebook Ads to Grow your Business

The advertising platform that is available on Facebook is designed in such a way that even people who have little to no digital marketing experience can create and run excellent ads.

You just need to learn the basics of Facebook ads and set up your accounts properly. Next, launch your campaign and then watch your business grow exponentially.

How to Convert with Facebook Ads

Facebook keeps on introducing new changes to its layout. It also changes the algorithm for News Feed quite often. Every little change in the algorithm is crucial for sellers who promote their products on Facebook, as you need to adjust your ads and advertisement strategy accordingly. This is especially true for people who own small-scale businesses and who do not have a large budget.

One of the crucial metrics that social media marketers track with the help of Facebook is the conversion rate. Conversion rates mean the point at which a general user becomes a buyer or a customer.

For many marketers, converting general browsers to customers is extremely important. If your service has a good conversion rate, it means that your business is successful.

Conversions are also responsible for driving action. The goal of any campaign is to increase the number of subscribers to newsletters. Ultimately, all the actions that can help your browsers become customers are conversion actions.

Facebook is considered to be the top most used social media website that creates a lot of conversions. To make the conversions even more effective, it is recommended to create effective and proper Facebook ads.

Here are some tips that can help you make your Facebook ad campaign a grand success.

1. Define Your Conversion Event

Before you try to convert users and regular browsers, you need to check out what actions you want people to perform once they interact with your ad.

Facebook supports many different kinds of conversions, including Add to wish list, view content, purchase, and initiate checkout. It also allows you to create custom conversion events as well.

If you create just one ad, do not expect it to cover all your bases. You need to create a separate ad for each individual goal. Target the ads carefully so that their sequence should make sense.

2. Keep the Destination in Front of Mind

An ad is closely related to its landing place. If your ad is exceptional, but your landing page is boring, the Conversion will not take place. If you genuinely want the Conversion to happen then make sure you make provisions that will help you deliver the promise you made in your ad.

Here are some tips that can help you make a proper landing page:

Pixel

Use pixel. Once you check the page where you want the Conversion to take place, you need to add the Facebook pixel code to the page. This will help you track the event.

Continuity

If your ad promises something, your landing page needs to deliver it. The customer should not have to look for the products that he or she saw in the ad. The design and language of the ad should be replicated on the landing page as well.

Optimized for Apps

A lot of people use their cellular devices to browse Facebook. Your ad should be optimized in such a way that it can be integrated with the app.

3. Create Eye-Catching Visuals

You need to make your ad as eye-catching as possible. First impressions matter a lot in the case of social media ads. If you add in proper design aspects, visual, and sound effects, your ad will stand out, and people will be attracted to it.

Try to keep the text limited. Use it as sparingly as possible and avoid it completely if you can. Instead of using a lot of text in the images, use images that are bold and attract the attention of the audience. If you still plan to use text in your image, you can use Facebook's Image Text Check tool. This tool will help you check the rating of your text to image ratio.

- Size: If your image has low resolution, it will not bode well with the customers.

- Videos and Gifs: Try to use videos and Gifs in your ads. Users are more attracted to moving imagery compared to stable and static imagery. As many people tend to use Facebook on mobile phones now, try to make vertical videos for mobile devices.

4. Keep Copy Short

Do not make long ads. No user will read the ads if it incorporates lengthy descriptions.

- Personal: Try to use personal pronouns in the ad. It will help you form a personal relationship with the audience and the brand. Do not use 'we' in the beginning. 'We' is better for returning consumers.

- Jargon: Try to keep your ads as simple as possible. Do not use unnecessary technical jargon that regular users may or may not understand.

- Brevity: Keep your text and ad as brief as possible. Too much text and information can be too intimidating for users. You can use the Hemingway app to keep things brief.

5. Include a Direct Call-to-Action

The main focus of conversions is about motivating people to do something. To do this, you need to incorporate a strong call-to-action in your ad. You should use strong verbs like Discover, Start, Find, and Explore in your ad. Your main goal should always be directing people towards your landing page.

If you want to drive people to subscribe or make purchases, use phrases such as 'sign up' and 'buy now' or 'free'.

6. Broaden Your Audience

When you plan to create an ad, try to use the "targeting expansion". This way, Facebook will work towards finding users who are similar to the "interest targeting section." It will help you reach a variety of people, and also help you create more conversions at a cheaper rate.

You can also create a Custom Audience to create more conversions. If you possess data sets such as email lists of the subscribers, you can upload it to Facebook. Facebook will use this list to find your existing customers. The list of existing customers can then be used to find a Lookalike Audience. This audience will be your new audience who have similar or the same interests.

7. Optimize for Conversions

It is crucial to check off the 'conversions' box on Facebook. This box is present in the "Optimization for Delivery" section in the Budget and Schedule form.

By clicking on this box, you can increase the effectiveness of your campaign. While it is not absolutely necessary, it is worth trying.

8. Choose the Right Ad Format

There are many different ad formats available on Facebook. It depends on your goals what kind of ad format you should use.

Here are a few things to remember while choosing the right format:

- Collection and carousel ads are ideal when you have several different features, services, or products that you want to highlight.

- Offer ads are great for letting people know about purchase incentives such as special offers, special discounts, and deals. Facebook will send the users notifications to remind them of these deals.

- Canvas ads are great for high-impact images and experiences that are best viewed on full screen.

9. Track across Multiple Devices

It does not matter where you have planned the Conversion to happen, you should still track all the conversions and clicks from mobile to desktop. Even if your campaign is solely focused on the desktop, it is recommended to install the Facebook Software Development Kit on your mobile. This will help Facebook to find more audience data and increase your target audience as well.

10. Consider Link Click Optimization

If you see that your ad is not creating enough conversions in the initial days, you should check whether Facebook is receiving enough data to properly deliver your ad or not. Facebook needs at least 50 conversions per ad in the first week. If your ad does not pull this many people, then there is something wrong with your ad.

To check how many conversions have happened, just click on the Ads Manager option. Here you will be able to check whether your ads have received less than 50 conversions.

11. Convert Your Analytics into Insights

It is necessary to pay close attention to the analytics of the social media campaign. You need to adjust your ads and marketing strategy according to the analytics. Pay close attention to the things that worked and the things that did not work.

Take notes from your old ads and try to incorporate the good things in your future ads and avoid the negative things from your previous ones.

Now that you know how to create and optimize a Facebook ad that is suitable for conversions, you need to focus on other social media sites and options that can help you market your products and Etsy store. It does not matter which platform you use, the experience of marketing will remain the same. You need to keep things direct, clear, enticing, and consistent.

CHAPTER FOUR

PINTEREST MARKETING

How to Promote Your Shop

People who use Etsy are definitely unique compared to sellers on other platforms. You need to use this uniqueness on other platforms as well. For instance, you need to adopt interesting methods of promoting your product and attracting customers to your shop. Pinterest is a great way to attract users to your shop on Etsy.

Many people use Pinterest for a variety of reasons, but most of us use it to pass the time. It is quite difficult to pull away from Pinterest because it is so addictive. You can browse things nonchalantly, or you can browse things to make plans.

Pinterest is great for Etsy sellers because users who look for your products on Pinterest are more likely to buy them. It is a great way to entice customers. It also focuses on special creative photos and uses a strong search engine. Pinterest can be used to promote your

Etsy store. Let us have a look at how you can use Pinterest to promote your Etsy shop.

How to Promote Your Etsy Shop on Pinterest

1) Create Great Visuals

While it is not a good thing to judge a book by its cover, it is what people tend to do all the time. People tend to judge things on a superficial basis. We judge products as well as accounts on the basis of visual cues.

To make your store and products popular on Etsy, you need to make them attractive, bold, and stunning.

- **Adopt a Pinterest "Style"**

One of the major things that can make your Etsy profile on Pinterest great is by choosing a theme and following it. You should align your themes and profiles in such a way that on whichever page the user lands, he should feel the cohesiveness.

All the pins should look like they are from the same family and that they belong together. This keeps things clean and attractive.

- **Maximize Space with Vertical Photos**

On Etsy, items are categorized in straight rows and columns, but in Pinterest, only the width of the image is limited. This means you create long vertical images. These long images not only look stunning, but they also help you cover a lot of information in one single image. These long pins can really make or break your profiles if you know how to use them.

2) Build a Pinterest Following

- **Curate Interesting and Inspiring Boards**

Etsy is quite a competitive marketplace, which is why many users tend to pin only their products on their Pinterest profile. But this can prove to be contraindicative to your desire. If you want your account to grow, you need to add a lot of Pins and curate your board carefully. Instead of curating just your products, you should curate stimulating and inspiring boards.

These should contain all the relevant trends, topics, and aspirations that people may find interesting. These boards should also be relevant to the style of your brand and the demographics of your customers. This will help followers of your Pinterest to become your customers.

Curating on Pinterest is quite an easy task. You should always use the 80/20 rough guide while doing it. This rough guide says that you should always add 80% of pins that your customers will find interesting, and the rest of 20% should incorporate your products that you plan to sell.

It is recommended to use as many pins as possible from the content of potential customers. You should try to keep your Pinterest as hopeful and cheerful as possible. Your Pinterest should inspire your potential customers to buy your products in a subtle but prominent way.

- **Curate Boards Useful to Your Customers**

You need to learn how to curate boards that will prove to be useful to your customers. For instance, if you sell knitted products, you can create a curated board for new parents who would like to care for their baby and wrap her in warm, soft, and delicate clothes. If you think that your products will be useful for parents doing newborn baby photography, curate boards dealing with photography tips and ideas. But, remember to maintain the unique style of your board and store. Your theme should not change.

If you are still worried about curating boards using other people's content, then just try to distinguish the content and content creators carefully.

Always try to share the content that you find relevant to Pinterest. It does not matter even if the content belongs to your competitor. It will still help you in the long term.

3) Embrace Getting Saves

A phenomenon that many people hate on Pinterest is 'Repin' where other people just share or pin our carefully created board with a strange heading. This is especially true in the case of Etsy sellers whose boards get pinned under 'DIY' or other similar tags. This is why many Etsy sellers try to avoid Pinterest.

The people who DIY regularly do not buy new stuff, but their followers do. For instance, if you Pinboard and DIY-er pin it to remake it, his or her followers may want the same product. And these followers may just check your link and buy the product quickly, because most of the time followers lack the patience, time, and skills for a DIY product.

Repin and other forms of pin engagement are good for your popularity as well because it makes your board popular in the Pinterest algorithm. The Pinterest algorithm is responsible for deciding what pins and boards are seen by everyone in their feeds. The more the number of engagement and Repins, the better the chances of your board showing up in the feeds of potential consumers.

4) Take Advice from Successful Etsy Sellers

You should try to contact and ask for advice from experienced Etsy sellers who have been using Pinterest to increase their business. As Pinterest is a large-scale platform, there are many tricks and tips that you need to figure out to use it in the best way possible. These experts can help you figure these tips out.

5) Think Like a Search Engine Marketer

One of the best things about Pinterest is that it is not only a marketing platform, but it is also a good search engine. People generally visit Pinterest because they are looking for something. This is why it is a great idea to promote your Etsy store of Pinterest. It will allow you to target your potential customer base by checking out what they generally search for.

Sit down and brainstorm the phrases and keywords that your customers may search for while looking for your products. You can also use the 'AutoSuggest' option to find simple keywords. To do this just type the first few initial letters of your query in the search box, Pinterest will automatically suggest the terms that are used the most.

Check out these results. These are important because they are your competitors. To succeed, you will have to make better Pins than these results.

Pin your descriptions with the keywords that you plan to tag. You need to create Pinterest boards that can target the categories of keywords that you find relevant.

6) Advertise on Pinterest

Pinterest is not only a good search engine, but it is also a good place for advertising. If you want to get almost immediate feedback on how your Pins are performing, you can check it using the Clickthrough Rate or CTR option of Pinterest. It is available in the Pinterest Ads Manager. According to PRs, you need to focus on campaigns that have 0.20% or higher CTR.

Once you check out which Pins are generating the most conversions and clicks for you, you can increase their budget and can reach even more people. One of the best things about Pinterest is that you can target people with ads on the basis of their searches. Generally, if a person searches for something, he or she is willing to buy it as well. It is no wonder that search marketing is so popular nowadays.

7) Be Consistent

Etsy and Pinterest both take time and patience. But the fruits of this patience are immense. You need to understand that building a good Etsy store and a Pinterest account both take time and effort. Your growth needs to be gradual but organic. You need to share good Pins constantly. You also need to grow your boards slowly but steadily. This will increase your audience.

By studying many different accounts, it was found that the accounts that share around 20-30 Pins every day grow significantly more than the accounts which share less or more than 20-30 Pins. Apparently, if you share more than 30 Pins per day, it will lead to negative effects, and you may start to see negative growth too.

Creating a Pinterest Profile

If you are not using Pinterest for business now, you should do it as soon as possible. You need to put in the ideas that will help you grow on this platform as this platform is rapidly achieving great success all over the world.

Pinterest is a great combination of a variety of options that make it a good platform for marketing. It is not only a good place to connect with your friends, but influencers as well. It also serves as a productivity tool and a visual search engine.

Pinners use Pinterest to find inspiration for a variety of things, be it vacations, bridal showers, weddings, holidays, or even simple luncheons. Many times these inspirations come through brands, which makes them popular. This section will help you understand the basics of using Pinterest for business and how you can use it to make your business a grand success.

Why Should You Use Pinterest for Business?

There are many reasons why you should use Pinterest for business to promote and market your Etsy shop. Pinterest is currently the fourth most popular social media platform in the United States. You will be surprised to know that it ranks ahead of stalwarts such as WhatsApp, LinkedIn, Snapchat, and even Twitter. It is believed that around 28% of American adults have a Pinterest account. This means that every one in four people in the US uses Pinterest. The number becomes even more striking when you consider the millennial population. Every one in two millennials in the United States has a Pinterest Account.

This, however, does not mean that Pinterest is only popular in the United States. It also plays a significant role in the world. From 2017 to 2019, the number of monthly active users (around the globe) grew by 38%. It went from 171 million to 235 million. This number will continue to grow. Since last year, the number of Pinners who use Pinterest at least once a month increased by a whopping 28%. Around 322 million people use Pinterest actively in a month.

Visual Search is Growing

Why is Pinterest growing so rapidly? The main reason behind the growth of Pinterest is perhaps the rise in visual searches. People are becoming more and more image-oriented, and they prefer to look at images rather than text. Pinterest is a 'visual discovery engine.' It is one of the most important platforms that offer visual search options. This is a big achievement. Around 62% of millennial and Gen Z population has accepted that they would rather search using images than text. According to Pinterest sources, Pinterest Lens is now capable of identifying more than 2.5 billion fashion and home objects.

Pinterest is Popular with Women—Especially Moms

This should not come as a surprise, but Pinterest is more popular among women compared to men. In fact, it is even more popular among moms. It is estimated that more than two-thirds of the users on Pinterest are women. The number of mothers on Pinterest is high as well. In the United States, around eight in every ten mothers use Pinterest regularly. This is good for your business if you deal with household and baby products.

People use Pinterest to Shop

Some 84% of weekly users use Pinterest to help decide what to buy. According to Pinterest, 55% of Pinners are specifically looking for products. And 83% of weekly users have made a purchase based on the content they see from brands on Pinterest.

Pins Boost Brand Exposure

Pinners have now realized that Pinterest is great for brand exposure. According to a recent survey, around 75% of users have agreed that they are interested in new products compared to the 55% of users who use other social media sites. Around 77% of total Pinterest users have agreed that they have discovered new brands in the past week using Pinterest. This does Pinterest a really lucrative service for small businesses and brands.

Pinterest Inspires People

Pinterest can also inspire individuals because it is ultimately a collection of plans and ideas. A whopping 95% of users have said that they have found inspiration on Pinterest in the past.

On Pinterest, unlike on any other site, a brand can become more than just a brand. It can become a source of inspiration and ideas for people.

Pinterest for Business: Important Terms to Know

Pinterest has its own language that you need to understand if you want to market your products successfully on the website. Here is a small glossary that will help you get started.

Pinner

Instagram users are known as 'grammers, and LinkedIn users are known as members. Similarly, users who use Pinterest regularly are known as 'Pinners.' It is the branded term that defines a person who uses Pinterest.

Pins

Pins are the primary kind of posts that can be uploaded on Pinterest. Pins generally incorporate videos, images, texts, and often link back to the original poster or the source of the content.

RePins

When a user pins a post that does not belong to him or her, this process is known as Repins.

Promoted Pins

Promoted Pins are just like regular pins, except companies pay a money to promote these pins. These pins are generally seen on both the feed and the search results. They include a 'Promoted' label. There are many kinds of promoted pins, such as app pins, video pins, and carousel pins.

Rich Pins

Rich pins are pins that contain a lot of information. It can include install buttons, price, and other such data. They are available in four types: Recipe Pins, Product Pins, App Pins, and Article Pins.

Shop the Look Pins

To add product tags to the creative, you need to use the Shop the Look pin. This allows users to buy whatever products they see in a pin with just a tap.

Boards

Pinterest boards are just like your regular old boards, except Pinterest boards are digital while the old boards are analog. You can collect and pin a lot of data related to various topics and themes on your board. For instance, you can create a mood board, a shopping board, an inspiration board, etc.

Group Boards

Group boards are just like regular boards, except in these boards, more than one user can add content. Generally, group boards only have around five members.

Secret Boards

Secret boards are visible only to the creator of the board and the collaborators whom the creator has invited. If you create a secret board, a lock sign will appear next to the board name. These boards are great for planning, which you may not want to do in front of the public. These are useful for planning.

Protected Boards

These boards are protected and then generally hold the promoted pins. These are only available to real advertisers. While these boards are seen all over Pinterest, they never come up on profile pages.

Save Button

As the name suggests, this button is used to save things. It is available as a browser plugin for Microsoft Edge, Chrome, and Firefox. You can install it on your website. Whenever a user clicks on the save button, he or she will be able to save the products on his or her Pinterest board.

Audience Insights

Pinterest business accounts can access your analytics using Audience Insights. This can help you learn a lot about how to use Pinterest and which sections of the site and your service you need to track.

Pinterest Lens

This is available for both Apple and Android devices. Pinterest Lens is an app-based tool that allows you to search for 'related' and 'relevant' content on the website by just clicking a picture using your phone. It is a kind of visual search engine like Shazam but devised specially for images.

Pincodes

Pincodes are, in a way, QR codes. They work just like Snapchat's Snapcodes. You can scan these digitally, or you can also scan them from packages, etc. These codes are linked to the user shops.

How to Set Up a Pinterest Business Account

There are three methods that you can use to create your Pinterest business account. These are:

- Converting your existing account to a business account.

- Adding a business profile to your personal account

- Creating a new business account

While the methods are different, most of the steps involved in these three are similar. In this section, let's have a look at how to create a new business account on Pinterest.

1. Visit Pinterest.com/Business/Create

Log out from your personal account. On the new page, click on email and add your new email ID. Create a new password and then click on Create Account.

2. Add your Business Name

Add a description that describes your business in the best way possible. Also, add a link to your website in this description.

3. Connect your Instagram, Etsy, YouTube Accounts

Link your Etsy, YouTube, and Instagram accounts to your profile. It will allow you to get traffic from all the sites. It will also help you track the analytics of your business.

4. Let Pinterest Know if You are Going to Put Ads on the Platform

If you want to run ads on your Pinterest account, it is necessary to specify contact details to the service. A rep will contact you regarding this soon.

5. Edit your Profile

Click on the pencil icon next to your name on the dashboard. You should also change your profile name because Pinterest automatically sets it to your email id.

Always put a photo that represents your brand thoroughly. You can use your logo for this purpose. The dimensions of this picture should be 165 x 165 pixels.

In the about section, do not forget to add a few keywords that represent you and your brand.

Click on the Save button to save your profile.

6. Click Claim in the Left-Hand Menu to Claim your Website

Claiming your website is essential. It will help you track your analytics. The next section will help you understand what claiming is, in detail.

7. Create a Pinterest Board

To create a board, just click on the plus sign above the Create a Board text. Next, add a description and title. Find the board and click on the pencil icon.

Choose the category of your board. This is important because it will help SEO. Be sure and add a good and relevant cover photo.

8. Create your First Pin

Creating your first Pin is an exciting and interesting experience. To do this, just click on the plus sign present on the upper right corner of your dashboard.

Next, add a description and a title. Remember to include relevant hashtags and keywords.

Also, add a destination link and click on it to check whether it works or not. Add a video or an image to the Pin. You can edit these by either adding logos, or cropping, or tripping. You can also add text to the Pin in the Pin editor. Use high-quality files to create pins.

Click on Publish and then select the board on which you want to add this Pin.

It is recommended to install the Pinterest save button as soon as possible. It will allow you to populate your boards from your favorite sites in no time. You can also use Pinterest catalogs.

9. Choose a Cover Photo for your Profile

Setting up a cover photo is simple. Just click on the pencil icon above the image. Pinterest will fill the section with creativity from your pins automatically. You can either choose between pin creative or board creative. According to some sources, businesses will soon be able to add videos as their covers.

10. Add the Pinterest Tag

If you want to advertise on Pinterest, it is recommended to add the Pinterest tag on your web page. It will allow you to track conversions and also help you understand what activities people do after visiting your page.

Now that you have successfully created your business account on Pinterest, you need to work towards attracting followers to your profile.

Using Pinterest for Business

In this section, let us have a look at the variety of tips and tricks that you can use to make your Pinterest marketing successful.

1. Create Captivating Content

The world keeps on changing rapidly, and if you do not have creative content, no one will bother to check your products. It was observed that around 85% of Pinners like images more than text. But this does not mean that you should only concentrate solely on images. Text is important, as well. At the end of the day, you should create well-crafted pins that deliver on all fronts.

What makes a good pin?

There are many things that make a good pin. Let us have a look at some of them:

Descriptive Copy

It should include information about what the users are viewing. It should attract them. Your content needs to be as enticing as possible.

Vertical Imagery

Almost 85% of Pinners use Pinterest on a cellular device. It is recommended to use a 2:3 ratio for your pins and images. This way, your image won't get truncated. Always try to use the highest quality available. Remember that Pinterest is a visual-centric social media.

Text Overlay

Try to use a headline in your pins so that you can reinforce your message properly.

Branding

Brand your pins carefully. They should not get lost if someone repins them.

Storytelling

If you can create a story through your pins, the customers will appreciate it a lot, and they will be far more interested in purchasing things from your store. Creating a story is one of the best ways to entice customers.

2. Pin Consistently

Social media is not a one off thing (unless you are a famous personality or brand.) It takes patience, effort, and time to grow. You need to pin something at least once a day. This is more effective compared to creating a board and filling it up all at once.

If you find yourself too busy to pin every day, just schedule them on Pinterest or a third-party service like Hootsuite. This will ensure consistency in your account. Do check Audience Insights from time to time and see which content is getting the most engagement. Try to post when most of your targeted audience is online.

3. Plan Ahead for Seasonal Content

Pinners are generally interested in unique products and DIY. This is why they tend to plan way ahead of time. This means that you, as a brand catering to Pinners, need to start planning in advance as well. It is recommended to start planning for seasons and holidays at least a month in advance. The earlier you start, the better.

Holidays and seasons provide great opportunities to brands all over the world. In 2018, more than 56 million searches were done on Pinterest. For Halloween, it was 227 million, and for December holidays, it was more than 321 million.

It should not come as a surprise that holidays can boost a brand's performance. According to Pinterest, promoted pins that are themed appropriately for holidays and seasons can increase sales by around 22%.

If you do not know how to plan for seasons or holidays, then just visit the Seasonal Insights Planner available on Pinterest. It will inspire you to formulate a proper plan. Next, pick a season or a holiday and create content around it. Be sure and use correct and relevant keywords while creating this content.

4. Use Boards to Connect with Pinners

Pinners will not follow you if you do not give them a concrete reason. Pinners need to find your Pinterest Board interesting. You can create a variety of boards to ensure this. Good and simple DIYs using your products will get you followers.

For instance, if you sell makeup products, you can create pins where you can show how to create particular looks using your cosmetics. You can also create boards incorporating various makeup tips, fashion ideas, new looks, experiments with makeup, etc. A good board will serve to be the launchpad for many influencers. These influencers will make your products and shop popular as well.

You can also use the group board to collaborate on ideas and boards together.

5. Optimize for Pinterest SEO

Users should remember that Pinterest is a visual search engine. Like any other search engine, Pinterest uses keywords so that it can look for things. This is why it is crucial to use keywords everywhere on your profile. You should use them in the pin names, companies, boards, etc. Remember to use keywords in the descriptions as well. Pinners often use Hashtags, which are a form of keywords.

Along with keyword research, you can also use other options that can help you with SEO. You can pin content from your webpage on your Pinterest page.

6. Create a Content Strategy that Delivers

Almost all the searches on Pinterest are non-branded. According to some sources, this number is as high as 97%. This gives new brands a lot of opportunities to get discovered. This is especially true in the case of brands that have good products and great content. If you pair this with SEO strategies, your brand will become popular.

Exposure is crucial, but for a good exposure, you need to create a good content strategy as well. You need to follow this content strategy carefully. Once a Pinner finds your products and your content interesting, you should add him or her to the marketing funnel so that you can turn their interest into a customer.

You should always reconnect with Pinners as soon as possible who interact with you. This will help you become a great seller. It will also lead to exponential growth in the popularity of your brand.

7. Target the Right Pinners with Ads

You need to learn how to target the correct demographics using Pinterest. Pinterest allows users to target ads that are created around keywords. These keywords are subjective to age, interests, location, and various other demographics. Audience targeting is a great option for advertisers and business owners because it allows them to reach difficult to reach groups. You can reach people such as people who have visited your website, people who have subscribed to your newsletter, people who have interacted with your pins, people who have interacted with similar content, etc.

You can also create an 'act-alike' audience that can help you find people who are interested in the same things that your customers are. The people who share the same interests are more likely to buy similar products as well. You just need to input an existing audience in the Pinterest algorithm, and Pinterest will find an 'act-alike' audience automatically.

8. Make it Easy for Pinners to Shop

Users who use Pinterest love to shop. Pinners are always on a lookout for new and exciting products. The sellers who make it easy to for pinners to buy their products experience greater sales compared to other sellers who do not try at all.

There are many methods to make things easier for buyers. One such method is using the Shop the Look pins. These pins contain specific home décor or fashion items that go well together. These pins link the customers directly to the products so that they can buy the things they like immediately.

A new 'Shop tab' is introduced by Pinterest, especially for business profiles. This tab allows interested Pinners to buy products from a company directly from their profile without having to visit their website. It is a new feature, but it is quite promising.

Remember, your business and Pinterest account; both can be improved if you pay close attention to Pinterest Analytics. Always keep an eye on the Audience Insights and change your plans accordingly.

If you find managing Pinterest difficult, there are many online services and apps that can help you manage things with ease.

Claiming Your Etsy Shop on Pinterest

Claiming your Etsy shop on Pinterest is important because it allows you to check the analytics and status of various things with ease. For many years, the only way a person could claim his or her Etsy shop on Pinterest was by accessing the back end of the website and by inserting some computer code in the process. But not anymore. Now it is possible to claim your Etsy shop on Pinterest with just a few clicks. The ease of this process has made things really good for buyers and sellers alike. In this section, let us have a look at the steps involved to claim your Etsy store on Pinterest. But before that, it is necessary to understand what claiming is and why it is important.

Claiming your account and linking it to Pinterest gives you a lot of good features. One of the major features that this process gives you is the attribution of pins to your Etsy shop. Your profile picture and Pinterest name get attached to the pin so that people can find you and trace things to your store with ease. The most important benefit claiming provides sellers is better to control over Pinterest Analytics.

Generally, analytics are shown on the pins I save to your boards from your store, but by using the 'claiming' option, the analytics will appear on all the items pinned across Pinterest accounts and boards. This allows you to see which users are pinning your products and where they are pinning them. Similarly, it also allows you to see how these pins are performing.

Let us now check out the steps that can help you claim your account.

Before claiming, you need to have a business account on Pinterest. Otherwise, you cannot claim your Etsy store. It is impossible to do so using your personal account. It is always better to have a business account, anyway. It is necessary for promotional reasons. Similarly, it offers you much better features as compared to a personal account.

Steps:

- Log in to Pinterest using your business account.

- Click on the three dots present on the upper right corner—select Settings.

- Click on Claim.

- You will be presented with a few options. Select Claim's other accounts, followed by Etsy.

- A screen will appear asking you to grant permission to your account to be connected to your Etsy account. Click on allow Access.

That's it! You have just claimed your Etsy account, and now your Etsy and Pinterest accounts are linked together.

Analytics

Whenever you come across a pin that was curated or saved from your store, stats will be displayed at the top of the page. These stats are only visible to you. They feature the details of the past 30 days.

If you want to see more details, just click on See More Stats link. You can also change the timeframe in this section.

The information received from these stats can be used to understand which demographics are pinning your products. You can also check in what context your products are being pinned. The boards will be quite varied, but you will see some DIY-focused boards. But even DIY focused boards will help you in the long term. You may also come across some exceptional boards that will help you plan your future strategy and adjust your pins accordingly.

Claim your Etsy account as soon as possible. It is also recommended to connect your account to Instagram as well. You should promote your content as much as possible. If you do not know how to use Instagram for business, the next chapter will help you understand the basics and the intricacies of Instagram.

CHAPTER FIVE

BUILDING A FOLLOWING WITH INSTAGRAM

Setting Up a Business Profile

Instagram has a lot of monthly active users. Some experts believe that this number is as high as 1 billion users. Instagram is no longer a niche social network and is now a social media mogul. It is one of the fastest-growing, most popular platforms that you should use to promote your business. If you don't have a business account on Instagram yet, create one as soon as possible.

Instagram is a visual-based social media platform where you post images and videos. It allows you to tell visually rich and graphically stunning and inspiring stories about your brand and business. Instagram is good for cross-posting content and can really help your brand to blossom.

How to Set Up an Instagram Business Account

Before beginning your Instagram journey, it is recommended to create a Facebook business account immediately if you do not have one yet. You cannot use Instagram's business account fully if you are not on Facebook. Once you create a business page on Facebook, you can go ahead and create a business profile on Instagram.

If you already have a Facebook business page, then move on and check out the step-by-step instructions on how to create and set up a business account on Instagram.

1. Download the App

To use Instagram, you need a mobile device. So, pull out your mobile phone and go to the app store to download the application. It is available on Google Play Store and IOS App Store as well. The overall layout and design of the app are the same across platforms.

2. Create an Account Using an Email Address

It is easy to create an Instagram account using your personal Facebook profile, but if you want to keep your personal and professional life separate, it is recommended to create one using your email address. Create your Instagram account using your business email. This way, you will be able to find people, and people will be able to find you with ease.

3. Profile Basics & Choosing a Username

Next, you need to choose a good password and username. The username should ideally be the name of your brand. If the name is already taken, try to use a name that comes as close as possible to the name you want. Remember to distinguish your name in such a way that people understand that it is a brand account.

Instagram generates an account name for you directly. If you do not want this to happen, just change the name in the settings.

4. Find Facebook Friends & Contacts

Once you create your account on Instagram, it will prompt you to find people via your contacts and Facebook. Before the following people immediately, it is recommended to set up your account and make a couple of posts. So, just click skip now, you can come back to this step later. This is not a one-time offer, so you can get back to that feature again and apply it.

5. Picking the Right Profile Photo

As you are planning to run a brand account, your profile picture should obviously display your brand logo. Later you can change it something else that is associated and recognizable with your brand. As this is not your personal account, do not use your selfie as the profile picture. Do not use any other group pictures as well.

Click on 'Add a photo.' You will be presented with a few importing options. Do not import pictures from Facebook if you have connected your personal account, as it will just pull your personal account info. You can pull information from your Twitter account if it is a brand profile.

Once you upload your profile picture, save your information. This will help you log in quickly next time.

If you do not want to save your login credentials, just click on skip.

Next, you will be presented with a list of suggests accounts to follow. You can skip this step as well, especially if the suggested accounts are not relevant to your business. For instance, if you sell vegan products and your suggested accounts are of barbeque places, avoid them, and do not follow them. Once you have made your decision, just click on 'Done' int eh upper right corner of the screen.

Once again, remember this is not a one-time offer, and you can always come back to this page later.

Quick Button Tutorial

Now that you have set up the app properly, you will be presented with a screen, which is your home screen. Once you follow other people's accounts, their photos will start to show up in your feed. In this section, let us have a quick run-through of various Instagram options and buttons.

Top Buttons:

- Camera: You can share photos and videos using this button.

- DM (Paper Plane): The paper plane symbol in the top right corner of the screen is your DM or Direct Messaging service. Here you can send and receive private messages. Use it carefully.

- Bottom buttons, from left to right:

- Home (shaped like a home): Clicking on this will bring you back to the accounts that you follow.

- Search (magnifying glass): Here, you can look up new people, accounts, hashtags, places, etc.

- Camera (addition sign): Here, you can upload pics and videos.

- Heart: Here, you can check the recent comments and likes of people on your posts.

- Profile (your photo): Here, you can check your profile and what things you have posted so far. It also allows you to access the settings menu.

6. Complete your Profile

Click on the profile button on the lower right corner of your account. Here select the 'Edit Your Profile' button. Here you can complete your profile.

Fill your contact information and bio carefully. Here you can also insert a clickable URL. Everywhere else, the URLs will be unclickable. This includes URLs posted in the caption of your photos or videos and comments as well. Do not waste time posting URLs here. URLs also work in DMs. If you want to direct people to your website, put your website URL in the bio section.

Your bio needs to be short and brief. It should contain a summary of where you are located and what do you do. If you cannot come up with the perfect bio immediately, write a decent one to start off and then go back when you have better ideas and change it.

7. Now Comes the Business Part!

Click on 'Try Instagram for Business Tools.' Follow the instructions that appear on your screen step by step. This will help you complete the profile; you can then use the tools carefully.

8. Link your Business Facebook Page

In the introduction to this section, the importance of creating a Facebook page for your business was mentioned. A business Facebook page is important because it will allow you to use business tools on Instagram. Instagram was acquired by Facebook a couple of years ago, which is why a lot of integration is seen between these two services now.

9. Start Posting

It is recommended to post a couple of posts on your account before the following anyone or asking them to follow you. People will not follow your account if they see nothing. A couple of photos that represent your brand will help you significantly.

10. Write Captions and Use Hashtags

Do not write too lengthy captions. Keep them brief and pair them with appropriate hashtags. Hashtags are not just for fun; they are important tools that can help your brand grow. They allow your content to be found with ease. Use targeted and specific hashtags instead of using generic ones such as #love, #sun, etc.

Do not add too many hashtags to your post. Instagram allows 30 hashtags per post, but it is recommended to use fewer than that, or your followers will feel bombarded.

11. Follow People and Get Social!

Now that you have completed your profile and have shared a few posts, you need to start following people so that they can start following you back as well. Click on your Profile page and go to the options page by clicking on the gear on the top right corner.

Here you can find two options: Facebook friends and Contacts. Click on both of these one by one, and Instagram will open your address book. Here you can follow people one by one. Once this is done, you can start following other accounts as well. Engage with their posts by commenting and sharing. This will help you create a large audience, and people will start to follow you back as well.

The more you comment and follow others, the more they will follow you back. You can check your comments, followers, and likes by clicking on the Heart in the bottom row.

12. Find and Define your Brand's Story

Once your Instagram profile is set and is ready, it is now time to decide the purpose of the account. Some brands use their business accounts to connect with their customers, while others use it to promote their products. Some brands also use Instagram to offer sneak peeks of their products, services, and brand. Choose wisely. You can also combine all these things to create a more inclusive and proper business account. Just try to maintain the cohesiveness of the account. Else your audience will get confused.

13. Get your Name Out There

Once your account is created, link your Instagram account everywhere. Similarly, add a link to your business in your Instagram profile as well. You should add your Instagram link to your email signature. You need to drive more and more people to visit your profile.

Branding

It is true that starting your Instagram business account from scratch can be quite difficult and daunting of experience, but it is quite rewarding as well. Many times brands start their Instagram with a lot of excitement only to stop working with dedication soon. These accounts then die out quickly, tarnishing the name of the brand. If you do not want this to happen, you need to be vigilant and dedicated.

If your account is already dead, this section has pro tips that will help you rejuvenate it. Creating a proper branding and marketing strategy is crucial if you want your business to succeed. Only dedication, patience, and hard work will help your brand grow.

Instagram branding is quite daunting, and many beginners find it really difficult because gaining attention and engagement of Instagram users, in the beginning, is a confusing and complex task. According to eMarketer, less than 50% of brands are genuinely active on the platform. The number may go up in the future, but it shows that there is much to learn about branding and marketing on Instagram.

Benefits of Increasing Instagram Branding

There around 1 billion active users on Instagram, which is why there are lots of opportunities to develop and grow your brand. More than 80% of active users check their feed at least once a day.

While you can always add paid ads on Instagram, you can also market your brand for free if you are dedicated enough.

Track Instagram Analytics

Instagram keeps on rolling out new features almost every month or so. There are many features available now that have made it a really great service for sellers and buyers alike. For instance, now, the seller can check links clicks in the platform itself. Yet, there is no way to collaborate, track, or view your Instagram metrics in one single place. But there are many third-party services and apps available that can help you do this. Using these services, you can view your total Instagram engagement with ease. You can even check how many people used your name and hashtags. These services can also help you check the hashtags trending in your industry right now.

How to Improve Branding on Instagram

1. Focus on Getting Real Followers

According to a study conducted by some Italian computer analysts, it was found that around 8% of Instagram accounts are either bots or act like bots. With this, they checked the number of defunct or inactive accounts, and it was found that around 30% of accounts do not post regularly or do not post at all. This means that the number of fake Instagrammers is going up day by day. These fake followers are bad for your business. These followers can throw a wrench in your plans of creating an engaged follower-base.

Inactive and spam-like bots can be avoided; you just need to focus on how to get real followers who are interested in your products and like to engage and interact with your brand.

Don't add followers just because you want to increase your follower count. While the quantity of followers is important, do not let the quality falter either. Instead of just increasing the number of your followers, try to increase your engagement with them and try to build a good connection with them. This can be done by posting questions that demand interaction.

Don't Deceive Your Audience

If your followers regularly share, comment, and like your posts, then you are in the right direction. But if your brand has thousands of followers who do no interact with your brand at all, then it means that your followers are fake and that you got them using some paid service. While the number of followers seems interesting in the beginning, your real audience will see through fake information. It will reduce your brand value.

Instead of risking things and paying for bot followers, you should try to build your brand steadily and gradually. Post at least one post per day and try to interact with at least 3 users every day. This will help you build your brand loyalty and awareness. It will show how you care about your followers and customers.

This is quite a demanding and time-consuming task, but it is immensely rewarding as well. Spend some time engaging your customers, and you will reap the benefits soon.

2. Place Your Emphasis on Beautiful Content

Instagram is a visual-based social media. To make your brand popular on Instagram, you need to create eye-catching and stunning content. If you use blank canvas with simple quotes, you will never get popular on the medium. You need to learn how to create engaging and attractive content. According to a study conducted by Forrester, it was found that Instagram is 10 times more engaging than Facebook. The number is even higher for Twitter, where it is 84 times more engaging.

Follow Basic Photography Tips

As said above, Instagram is a visual medium, which is why you need to concentrate on creating stunning visuals. Good visuals will help you engage more and more people. To create good visuals, you do not need to be a professional photographer with expensive gear. You can also create great visuals using your phone as well. You just need to follow some basic tips and methods of photography. In this section, let us have a look at some tips that can make your photos pop and your Instagram account popular.

Light

Photography is impossible without light. You need to set lights carefully if you want to click stunning photos. Do not invest a lot of money on lights and other such gear if you are a new brand. Instead, try to use natural light as much as possible. Avoid using overhead lights because they create unnecessary shadows. Always add light from the side, but try to use a lot of it. Bright images are more engaging because they 'pop.'

Subject

The positioning of the subject is important. Generally, your eyes look in the middle of the picture. It is necessary to put your product in the central area of the picture. Focus on your model or your product as much as possible. If your picture contains leading lines towards your central subject, then congratulation, you have created a successful image.

Imagine

Whenever you click an image, think of how it will look on Instagram. Instagram does not allow pictures of all dimensions. Check the dimensions of your image beforehand. It is recommended to use the rule of three to maintain the shape and dimensions of your image. You can divide your image into 9 equal squares to check whether your image fits or not. Nowadays, there are many apps that will let you do this with ease.

Shapes and Colors

Try to use bold, beautiful, and bright colors. Your colors should not only reflect your brand, but they should also look stunning. If you do not plan to use colors, create high contrast black and white images. These images will stand out and look stunning.

Another way to make your black and white images stand out is by using various shapes and silhouettes in your photography. These things can make huge differences and can make your images look amazing.

Editing

Photography is one part of clicking images and two parts editing. If it is impossible for you to hire professionals, use some good editing apps to edit your photos. Do not use too many filters, though. Try to keep things simple and attractive as you are trying to attract followers and not win a photography contest.

3. Post Content Your Audience Actually Likes

Good content can help you engage a lot of users. You need to make your content not only relevant but pretty as well. You need to post content that your audience will like. A lot of users like to follow various brands on social media, especially on Instagram. If you can let your brand and aesthetics shine through your posts, it will help you create a strong and honest audience who would love to buy products from you all the time. Always think of what content will your audience likes and want. Finding what your audience likes and wants is quite easy nowadays, thanks to various insights options available.

Get More Audience Insights

The quickest and one of the best ways to get insights about what your audience likes is by asking them questions. Ask your followers frequently about what kind of content they would like to see. Most of them will surely let you know what they want. If you do not want to engage with your audience in this way, you can also use other methods. For instance, you can use social media analytics tools through which you can check the engagement of each post individually.

It is possible to get a lot of insights about your content and its performance using these tools. There are many insights tools available in the market now. Use them wisely. These tools will help you curate your content carefully. It will help you see which kind of content gets the most engagement and traction and which content is a dud.

4. Create Your Own Style

To become successful in the world of social media, you need to be creative, bold, and unique. You need to attract the audience by being as creative as possible. Only this will help you increase your visibility on Instagram. You need to create a style and an aesthetic of your own (or your brand). The style should be so unique that any person should be able to recognize it and associate it with your brand.

To understand how styles and themes work, just check the account of any major brand. You will able to make out a unique and interesting style. Use these styles as templates to design your own.

For instance, many 'Goth' jewelry stores tend to use dark and 'Gothy' themes. All the posts and videos tend to be on the darker side, which helps to create an aesthetic look that is not only in accordance with the products but also appealing and pleasing. Users will understand what you are trying to sell immediately once they see your posts.

Another great example of this is Harley-Davidson. The world-renowned brand of motorcycles uses a lot of metal, wood, and similar earthy tones in its posts. This gives it a typical and iconic theme and aesthetics.

Taco Bell, too, has become quite popular because it is highly active on social media. Taco Bell uses vibrant and bright colors. This look helps it target young customers. While Taco Bell uses its themes and aesthetics all over the Internet, you can observe how the brand utilizes it on Instagram for inspiration.

Before you create a branding strategy for Instagram, it is recommended to check out your competitions. Check what kind of brand value they have and what themes and aesthetics they are using. Try to utilize a style that speaks to your audience and you because originality matters a lot, especially to the young audience. Keep things simple but original.

5. Start a Hashtag Campaign

Hashtags are really important in the world of social media and especially Instagram. On Instagram, hashtags can be used to get masses speaking about your products, brand, and service. According to a survey, around 70% of the most popular hashtags on Instagram are branded.

Generally, brands use two hashtags per post. Hashtags can be quite elaborative, but they can be as simple as the name of the brand itself. Using hashtags, a company promotes its brand. Hashtags can also help you interact with your audience.

It does not matter if your follower count is low; if your hashtag becomes popular, people will get your products. This is why it is always recommended to start a hashtag campaign. There are many reasons why you should start a hashtag campaign, such as trying to make people familiar with your product, or finding new customers, etc.

Hashtags allow masses to get involved in your business and brand. It is a great way to build your brand from nothing.

6. Avoid Hard-Selling Language

While almost all the demographics use Instagram now, it is still the most popular in the 18 to 29 years age range. This age group generally does not trust brands on social media. They are hesitant to buy new things from the brands that appear on social media. According to research, around 30% of millennials in the United States of America are skeptical or scared about buying things from brands because of their selling and branding methods.

This does not mean that millennials do not like online shopping, rather millennials love to buy things online. Millennials are just off-put by the strange and over the top marketing strategies that many brands on social media tend to use. They can sense dishonesty in these ad campaigns. If your target audience is millennials, be as honest and open as possible. Do not try to full them. Do not try too hard.

As said above, use good videos, images, and content. It will help market your products to the target audience properly. Adding good captions to your posts is necessary as well. These captions are essential because they help users understand more about you. Do not ignore captions, as posts with no captions may appear insincere.

But adding captions to your posts is an art. You should never overdo it. Your caption should only include the important details, and these details should be prioritized. Instagram allows you to post captions that are 2,220 characters long, but it is recommended to be brief. No one likes to read too long of a post. Get to the point immediately and make your users read the posts, Instagram is not your blog, so don't write long-winded posts.

Pro Tip: You can increase the interest of users by using content that you know works. Just check which of your posts have been the most successful and which of them have received the most engagement. Check why they received the most engagement and try to replicate the reasons in the next post.

7. Cross-Promote Your Instagram

Many marketers use Instagram as their second or even third social media outlet. If you already have a social media channel on Facebook or any other social media site or app, you can use it to cross-promote your channel and product.

It is difficult to find ads that do not contain a Facebook link or a Twitter profile. Instagram is becoming more and more popular now because it allows content to be shared on various platforms, including Facebook and Twitter.

It is a good idea to build your marketing strategy by cross-promoting. This will help you build your brand over multiple channels, including Instagram. Some people believe that cross-promoting can be counterproductive and that it can hurt your traffic on all the channels, but in reality, cross-promoting has more pros than cons.

Cross promoting can help you drive your audience towards the funnel. You can provide your audience with a great experience that they will enjoy a lot, all thanks to cross-promoting.

Cross-promotion is great if you want to funnel customers. It is also good if you want to check out a variety of sources to spread your content.

Instagram allows only one link in its bio. So some people find it difficult to funnel their customers. This is why cross-promoting is essential on Instagram. By cross-promoting your Facebook, LinkedIn, Twitter, etc. you will be able to build a larger audience, and you will enable a chance to your customers to check out your content at their ease.

8. Showcase User-Generated Content

You should try to use content generated by users on Instagram. This is great for businesses and brands. According to a survey, it was found that more than 84% of millennials trust this kind of content and are more likely to buy from a brand that uses these methods. It can play a crucial role in deciding the purchase of items.

Only 35% of users who use social media trust brands. Around 65% of users still feel some hesitations while approaching business. The UGC

- Contest winners

- Account takeovers

- Celebrity content

- Everyday users with your brand

- Influencer reviews

It is crucial to understand that UGC can be quite problematic because if you do not ask permission of users before using their content on your page, you may land into legal trouble.

If you plan to allow account takeovers, then you need to be cautious about them as well. They may alienate your audience if the person taking over your account is not good enough.

In the initial stages of your Instagram branding process, just try to remember why you are on Instagram and try to find as many new people as possible. Do not host any random contests with random prizes. Instead, try to build trust and faith by engaging with people in a wholesome manner.

9. Make sure everything is Cohesive

Cohesiveness makes advertisements extremely lucrative. For instance, if you are trying to sell 'Goth jewelry' and you market it to small children or the elderly, your advertisements and products both will be inconsistent and incohesive. The same can be said about social media too.

On social media sites, like Instagram, your brand should be cohesive. So, if you use any logo or text on your videos and images, just be sure that these things follow the guidelines of your brand. Do not give away the guidelines of your brand. Make everything including fonts, colors, and overall aesthetics match with your brand

For instance, if you sell vegan products, try to incorporate a 'vegan' aesthetic in your posts. Build a theme and follow it.

In the initial days, do not hurry or rush while posting things on your feed. Take things slow and check whether your prospective posts match with your brand and theme. They should be coherent. If you post off-brand stuff right in the beginning, it can cause a problem with your future prospects. It may slow down your growth as followers may find your brand untrustworthy.

124

10. Test Everything

When you start using Instagram in the beginning, it is recommended to test everything out, including your content as well. For instance, in the case of the network alone, you should test things including

- Hashtags

- Bio Links

- Instagram Filters

- Post captions

- Call to actions

- Post apps (Boomerang, Hyperlapse, etc.)

- Types of content (video or images)

It is true that this may seem to be too much work in the beginning, but it will allow you to find the right balance between your content, which increases your reach and number of followers as well. Instagram changes rapidly, and so do the trends present on it. You need to update yourself from time to time if you really want to be successful on Instagram. Trying out new things will help you stay updated.

You can use various methods that can help you stay updated. There are also many third-party apps and sites that can help you enhance your followers and keep your profile updated.

11. Engage, Engage, Engage!

If you want to be successful on any social media site, you need to engage with your followers as much as possible. You cannot create a team of loyal followers if you do not engage with them. Your engagement will help your audience understand that you are not only patient but quite helpful as well.

The world is changing rapidly, and more and more people are now using social media to find a new product, new brands, and new services as well. Similarly, sellers all around the world are using different forms of social media to attract new customers and target the old ones as well. You need to make your brand ready for these updates and changes. Use the above-mentioned branding tips to keep your profile and advertisements updated.

Chapter Six: Email Marketing

Setting Up an Opt-In Page

In the world of social media and rapid marketing, email marketing may seem quite odd and useless to many people, but this is false. Email marketing works really well. It is still the best way to convert users.

The process of email marketing begins even before you send your first mail. You need to get people on your email list before you start sending emails. This can be done with ease by setting up a landing page that can convince people to sign up. These land-in pages can be quite great if you know how to be convincing and coercive without appearing too brash and desperate. You need to win the trust of people if you want them to subscribe to your email. In this section, let us have a look at some tips that can help you get started.

Tips:

Who do you want?

In this step, you need to think of your target audience. You need to come up with some ideas about what kind of people do you want on your list. You need to have a clear understanding of things to make a proper list. Without a proper and clear understanding of whom you want on your list, you will not be able to form a message that will resonate with people properly. Your message should be able to not only enhance the interest of people, but it should also help you gain their trust.

Aiming the message carefully at the right person is a skill that you need to learn if you want to do email marketing successfully.

Take your time to think of everything and figure it out. If you really want to create a good list that will cover everything, you need to think a lot from the point of view of the customer and the seller as well. Only start email marketing when you learn how to speak the language of your customer.

What do you want them to do?

Your email opt-in page should be opt-in page only. The only motive of this page should be to get people to sign up for your email list. It should not do anything else other than asking people to sign up for your email list.

Each little element and every word on the page should only focus on this action. If you add anything else to the page, the purpose of the page will be lost. So, do not add your regular links or sidebar to the page. Create a page that is only focused on one thing and ignore everything else. Your approach towards this page should be different than any other page of your store.

What are the essential elements?

Your email opt-in page needs to have these following things:

- Headline: You need to come up with an exciting headline.

- Benefits: You need to tell the benefits of your program and products in simple bullet points.

- Call to action: You need to convince people and tell them expressly to sign-up.

- Opt-in Form: You need to add a section where they can actually opt-in.

- Proof: You should add some sort of social proof. This may include testimonials, subscribers, media mentions, reviews, etc. *

* The addition of proof depends on the number of criteria. If the strength of your brand is high, then you can add it.

What incentive should you give?

The incentive is like an ethical bribe. It is given to people to convince them to do something. You can offer some incentives to your followers to get them to sign up for your email subscription.

These incentives may include audio seminars, webinars, free reports, or any other freebie. These offers should be instantly gratifying, though.

This strategy works perfectly fine in many fields, but in others, thanks to the rise of technology, not many people 'fall prey' to it. Your email directly goes to the spam folder in such cases. The best way in such cases is to focus on the incentive carefully. You can offer a 'broken down' incentive. This can include parts of video or books, etc. People should understand that you are giving them more than what you are offering.

How long should your copy be?

Your copy should only be as long as it is necessary. Do not add random data to your copy. When designing an opt-in page, you need to have at least these three things: Benefits, Headline, and Call to action. But you can add more things by thinking of other things to add by checking what your target audience may need.

Do remember to add a reminder letting your subscribers know that you respect their privacy and that you will not share their private data.

How much information should you ask for?

The less data you ask from people, the more likely they are to sign up for your subscription service. People are more likely to subscribe to a service that only requires their email address as compared to a service that asks for their name and email ID. This shows how even something as simple as 'name' can reduce the number of your subscribers.

But do not change your format if you absolutely need some data from your subscribers. For instance, if your business requires name, phone number, and email id of your subscribers, then you must add it to your form.

Build trust, as it will help people to open up to you. This way, you will be able to communicate with people on a regular basis.

What works better?

All the above tips have been tried and tested for many years, and they work. But email listing is a subjective task that changes according to you, your business, and your target audience as well.

You need to adjust your button colors, headlines, and many other tiny tweaks. These things may increase your opt-in rate.

Ultimately you need to tweak your landing page as much as possible to make it perfect. Having a good opt-in rate is necessary, but it does not mean that you should attract people who are not relevant to your business. Your opt-in page and email marketing should be a target to only those people who will buy something from you. Remember all the steps and follow them carefully.

Setting Up An Autoresponder

What is an email autoresponder?

An email responder is a form of email marketing technique. It is automation software that sends an already written message to the contacts on your list. This sending of emails is triggered when the contacts fulfill a condition that is predefined. There is a multitude of conditions available, including birth dates, cash purchases, etc.

There are many reasons why you should set up an email autoresponder.

- It helps you save a lot of time and effort.

- It can help you create and maintain a good relationship with your contacts.

- It nurtures leads.

Gone are the days when people thought that autoresponder is only meant for big companies. Now anyone can set up an autoresponder. There are many affordable options available on the market. Nowadays, you can also find many free options that come with limited features, use them wisely.

What is the purpose of an email autoresponder?

There are many reasons why you should use an autoresponder.

- To send important messages to your contacts even when you are not around.

- To send important messages to your contacts without having to do it manually.

- Lead people towards the funnel.

- Send custom and tailored messages to specific groups in your list.

- Create income by driving conversions and engagement.

Examples of when an autoresponder is used:

- Sending discount codes.

- Sending special offers.

- Sending welcome emails.

- Sending reactivation emails.

- Sending abandoned cart emails.

How does an email autoresponder work?

Using an autoresponder is easy. You just need to write your email and then schedule it. The message will get sent on its own. If you use the right software, you will be able to send these emails without any problem.

To send these emails properly, you just need to create a proper automation marketing workflow. You need to set up some rules that will then 'trigger' the software to send the message automatically.

Next, you need to define an entry point for your workflow. This means that you need to set up a specific situation or a condition that will trigger the workflow and set it in motion.

Next, you need to check which trigger conditions are still to be answered in the workflow. Target them and add actions for them.

Once everything is done, you just need to check the order as well as the frequency of the emails. For instance, in the case of new subscribers, you should send a 'welcome' email in the beginning, followed by other crucial emails in the next weeks.

What to Write in an Autoresponder

An autoresponder is important if you want to go out and do not want to lose business. If you plan to stay away from your office for a while, it is important for you to set up an autoresponder. It is a crucial email-marketing tactic, as well.

An autoresponder message is a notification that people receive when they try to contact a person who is out of the office or who is unavailable. These messages generally contain some sort of information that helps the person sending the email.

These messages generally include:

- How long will the person be unavailable?

- Dates and duration

- Whom should people contact when the person is unavailable

- When will the person return

The Kind of Messages You Shouldn't Send:

You should not mix personal life with professional life. Whenever you communicate with people for business purposes, you need to be professional. Never send messages like:

'I am not in town now. I am out of my mind, and I really don't want to talk to you all. Contact me later when I get back. Bye and enjoy.'

This is an inconsiderate and childish message that many people will find offensive. If you plan to send such messages, then stop immediately.

If you are confused about what kind of messages you should send to people, don't worry. Here is a short list of samples of autoresponders that will help you create a good and professional autoresponder message. Use these as blank templates. Make necessary changes wherever you want. Try to personalize these messages for added effects.

Example 1

[Your Greeting]

Thank you for your email. The store is closed for the holidays. It will reopen on (date). Meanwhile, if you need immediate assistance, please contact us on (phone number). Sorry for the inconvenience.

Best Regards,

[Your Name]

Example 2

[Your Greeting]

I will be unavailable from (date) to (date). Please contact my partner for immediate assistance.

Kind Regards,

[Your Name]

Example 3

[Your Greeting]

Thank you for your message. I will be unavailable for some time. If you require immediate help, please contact (alternate person). If you do not need immediate assistance, I will get back to you as soon as I return.

Warm Regards,

[Your Name]

Example 4

[Your Greeting]

Thank you for your email. I am not in the office currently, and I have no email access. I will be back on (Date of Return).

Meanwhile, if you need immediate assistance, please contact my phone (number).

Kind Regards,

[Your Name]

Example 5

[Your Greeting]

Thank you for your email. I am not available this week. Please contact (Contact person) in case of an emergency.

Best,

[Your Name]

Example 6

[Your Greeting]

Thank you for your message. I will not be available from (Date) To (Date). Please contact (Contact Person) for urgent matters.

Best Regards,

[Your Name]

Example 7

[Your Greeting]

Thanks for your email. Your message is important for the company. I will respond to you soon.

Thank You!

[Your Name]

Promote New Products

When you start selling a new product or a service, you are highly excited about it. You want to promote it and want people to buy it. But there is often a question in the back of the mind of a new seller as to whether or not his or her product will sell. If it does sell, then great, but if it does not, there are many tricks that can be used to sell the products.

Email marketing is a great way to sell and promote products and services in the digital world. Many researchers have come out and have proved that email marketing really works. Learning email marketing and how to promote your products using emails is not difficult. In this section, let us have a look at how you can promote your product with emails.

Marketing automation is a great way to run your marketing campaigns online. They can help you promote your product with ease. If you plan and execute things properly, you can target your prospective audience and also deliver your message to the audience correctly.

In this section, let us have a look at how you can promote your new products using email marketing efficiently.

To begin, you need to design a promotional campaign before you start promoting your product. Your promotion campaign needs to familiarize and tease your contacts (subscribers) about your upcoming project. It should give sneak peeks to your new plans. It should give you some details about what you are about to offer in the future. This way, a sort of anticipation will be created in the mind of your subscribers.

1. Making a Good Campaign is Not Difficult

Your campaign should include:

- Create interest in the minds of people.

- Disclose information about the main features of your products.

- Create anticipation about the launch of your product.

- Motivate people about your product. They should feel interested in ordering your product.

- Ask them to provide feedback.

- If you do this properly, your loyal and honest customers will wait for your next big announcement.

It is recommended to launch your products around the time and dates when your audience is already quite engaged and active. This may include holidays, vacations, special occasions, days, etc.

2. Plan and Create Content for the New Product

If you want to launch and lead a successful promotional campaign, you need to create good content around your product. This content should be able to provide all the necessary and relevant information about your product to your customers. It should also be able to create some curiosity and anticipation about your product. You should be able to explain why it is necessary to buy your product. You should be able to show why it is useful and how it can help your customers.

You can also launch workflow with the help of emails and various other means and methods.

You need to decide what kind of content, emails, landing pages, etc. you need to incorporate in your plan. It should be created carefully. You should have a proper goal even before you start your marketing. Always ask yourself what the purpose of your marketing strategy is. The goal should always be related to the promotion of your service and product. It should always send out information about your Etsy store.

Your content should:

- Help you build a good contact list

- Reach the target audience

- Inform your contacts about the pros of your products and why they should use it.

- Inform your contacts about the various functions of your products.

- Build brand awareness and make your brand successful

- Inform people about how your product solves problems and helps them.

- Increases pre-order sales.

To prepare content, it is necessary to refer to various data available about your products and industry. You should also refer to news items and articles that will help you collect information. Use this information and incorporate it into your emails to your subscribers as well. This will help you create a good marketing strategy.

If your product is new and unique, it is necessary to promote in such a way that it should be the focus of your campaign. Do not talk about your old products unless absolutely necessary. Also, do not talk about things that you have already discussed or of things that your contact already knows.

Keep your message and emails as clear and lucid as possible. Include a call to action in each and every email. This will increase the interaction and impact of your emails.

Keep your messages relevant.

3. Present the New Product or Service From Every Angle

If your new product has a multitude of uses, you can promote it in a variety of ways possible as well. You can even create a series of emails to target and expose the variety of uses of the product.

If you want to let people know about the benefits and features of your product, just send a simple and short message. This will make the message more memorable and comprehensible. You should direct the messages towards groups of recipients carefully.

You should display the advantages, features, and benefits of the product. To assure people that your product fulfills their expectations and needs.

4. Solicit External Reviews

External opinions and reviews can be great for your business and marketing. It enhances and improves your credibility. You should send some samples or demos of your products to people who are on the top levels in your field. Ask them to review and test your products. Opinions of these people will help your products get more popular. These opinions will help people who are on the fence and push them towards buying your products.

If you are into the cosmetic and personal care business, you can also contact bloggers and YouTubers to review your products. If you do not know how to incorporate YouTube into your business, just contact the YouTuber, he or she will help you.

5. Prepare a Special Offer for Subscribers Only

Email marketing allows you to stay in (personal) touch with your consumers. If you execute email marketing properly, you will be able to create really good and long-lasting relationships with your customers. But remember, long-lasting relationships are built on trust only, and the trust needs to be mutual if you want the relationship to succeed.

If you create your contact list carefully, you will be able to interact with people who are really interested in your products and services. You can then give special offers to a select few of these by forming an 'elite' club.

Show your subscribers that you care about them by sending them unique offers that cannot be found anywhere else. This may include freebies, coupons, messages, products, etc. Personalized products are another great way to show people that you care.

You should contact only a chosen few about this, though. The offer needs to be exclusive. To do this, you can add caveats like 'only for the first 10 subscribers', etc. This will help you get quality subscribers in no time.

6. Diversify your Marketing

It is recommended to come up with a good and well-thought strategy before starting your email marketing chain. Along with this, it is also recommended to change your strategy from time to time and update it often. You should be able to distribute relevant information to people properly. Your marketing strategy should create a buzz about your products and brands everywhere.

Careful planning and diversified marketing strategies will help you get great and promising subscribers and, ultimately, honest customers.

CONCLUSION

Etsy is one of the best sites for small business owners who want to sell their unique and often handmade products to customers directly. It provides a multitude of options that make the whole process easy and affordable to sellers and buyers alike. While there are many stores on Etsy, not all of them can be called successful because not many stores employ marketing strategies while selling.

A seller needs to be a good marketer if he or she ever wants to own a successful business. Etsy is no different. You need to market your store and your wares if you want to be successful. If you are confused about how to market your shop, then just use the tips and tricks given in this book, and you will see the difference!